IMAGES
of America

KNIGHTDALE

IMAGES
of America

KNIGHTDALE

W.A. "Billy" Wilder and Wanda Ramm

ARCADIA
PUBLISHING

Published by Arcadia Publishing
Charleston, South Carolina

Library of Congress Control Number: 2013933914

For all general information, please contact Arcadia Publishing:
Telephone 843-853-2070
Fax 843-853-0044
E-mail sales@arcadiapublishing.com
For customer service and orders:
Toll-Free 1-888-313-2665

Visit us on the Internet at www.arcadiapublishing.com

*To all of the volunteers who have given and continue
to give selflessly to grow Knightdale*

CONTENTS

ACKNOWLEDGMENTS

Thank you to all who have helped with furnishing images, scanning, and gathering information. In particular, thank-yous go to Gary McConkey, Hugh and Mary Jo Cashion, Wayne Schulz and the Knightdale Historical Society, and the 1980s Heritage Council, which began this collection.

INTRODUCTION

In 1701, surveyor and adventurer John Lawson mapped the area that would become Wake County. According to records from the Knightdale Historical Society, he surveyed the area along the Neuse River. He recorded that the territory from the falls of the Neuse to what is now Knightdale "harbored vicious Indians." Lawson noted large numbers of panthers and abundant wild game. Records show that about a year later, he was tortured and killed by some Tuscarora Indians. After the Tuscarora War in 1711, the tribe was moved north.

The area became largely land granted by the British monarch, mostly to John Hinton. According to Charles Silver, Hinton's first land grant of 136 acres was eventually increased until it constituted about 22,000 acres. The grants reached from today's Rolesville on the north to Archer Lodge on the south. The area consisted of Johnston (formerly Craven), Orange, and Cumberland Counties. Wake County was carved out of these three existing counties. The first structure was the John Hinton house, constructed at Panther Rock.

From the beginning, the Hintons were active in politics. When the struggle for American independence began, John Hinton prepared his men to march against the British. He and the Wake Militia fought in the Battle of Moore's Creek Bridge and participated in the adoption of the Halifax Resolves.

At his death, Hinton bequeathed his plantations to his sons—Hardy, William, John, and Malacie. Whether the plantations were already named is unclear, because he did not supply the names in his will. They are known today as the Oaks, Midway, and Beaver Dam Plantations, in addition to Clay Hill. Plantation owners built churches as part of the Church of England, but the slaves attended Hephzibah Church near Wendell. The original building has been restored, and the church buildings in use today stand across the road. The plantation owners farmed the land and built schools.

The end of the Civil War brought drastic changes to the farming operations on plantations, due to the lack of labor. The plantations were largely dismantled, either voluntarily or as a result of tax problems. The lure of productive soil and available land brought an influx of families. Most moved in from Virginia, with some coming from eastern and western North Carolina. They included names familiar to this day—Knight, Smith, Griffin, House, Robertson, and Pair. In addition, Needham Jones moved in from Craven County, but he did not remain in the area past 1917. These newer residents bought land from the dismantled plantations and developed sizeable holdings. Reuben Wilder purchased the Jones land and raised 10 of his 14 children there.

The people who moved in from western parts of the state were drawn by the available pine timber. Sawmill owners and lumber merchants, like the Stameys and Ramseys, saw the prospect of good economic gain. Native pine trees, often as large as three feet in diameter, were abundant.

Those moving from Virginia or from eastern North Carolina were looking for good farming soil. Knightdale sits on the break between the Piedmont and the coastal plain. This location features gently rolling land characterized by fertile loam soil, with spots of Cecil red clay and some sandy soil. Farmers quickly found that the area produced good crops of all types. The earliest main crops were cotton and corn. Later, tobacco became the main cash crop, especially after the boll weevil infestation made cotton unprofitable. Soybeans and small grains filled in the acreage not planted with cash crops.

Seeing the need for better access to goods and transportation, as well as a better means of selling farm products, Henry Haywood Knight pursued a railroad station for the area. The Raleigh & Pamlico Sound Railroad Company gained right-of-way from Knight and Needham Jones and their wives for $1 in 1904 and began laying tracks. In 1905, Norfolk & Southern Railroad bought the Raleigh & Pamlico Sound Railroad Company, and the area began growing. Knight died in 1904 without seeing the railroad in operation. Bettie, his widow, had a survey completed to establish lots for the town. Her husband had presumed these to be future business locations, but most of them became residential.

The town, named Knightdale in honor of Henry Knight, became a prosperous community largely because it became accessible. Farmers could ship timber and other crops. People could arrive more quickly than when their only modes of travel were walking or traveling by horse. Mail required less time to reach its destination. Merchants could receive goods more efficiently, allowing stores to maintain a better flow of stock.

The community progressed with modern advancements. Knight's Chapel Church moved to Main Street and began to grow. A three-room school began furnishing a good education for local children. The train depot itself was a thriving business. Life's needs were being met. Community health improved with the arrival of Dr. Joseph Hester. Whether in his office across the path from his home or out making house calls, the doctor provided a valuable service.

With the birth of the town, volunteerism took root. Groups like the Women's Betterment Association for Knightdale Schools volunteered many hours to feed students hot lunches. They grew cotton to help provide money to help the schools purchase needed items. That spirit of helping continues with the PTA and PTSA. In 1940, a fire devastated the business district. Residents fought back, trying to stop the fire and helping to rebuild. Each time a need developed, local people worked to meet it. Whether thawing a water line or helping harvest a crop, residents were willing to grow the town. World War II disrupted life, as most of the able-bodied men were away fighting. Dr. Rupert Weathers doubled as mayor to help the town meet its needs.

Those women of the Betterment Association were the pioneers of the Home Extension Club. Volunteers formed a fire department and a rescue squad. The library operated with volunteers. Civic groups like the Jaycees and the Lions Club helped mentor youth and raise money for civic causes. That spirit existed in businesses as well. Who could have foreseen all that would develop because some people wanted to help?

One

BEGINNING AND SHARING

The earliest residents, other than the Tuscarora Indians, were the Hintons. Though an unfamiliar notion today, land granted by the king was a path to ownership in the 1700s. Grantees became involved in the area and helped further its progress.

In the next few years, new residents arrived, and they became involved in local life, which in turn improved from their efforts. Plantation owners divided and sold their vast holdings, providing new residents with places to live and farms to work. Time and need brought about many changes, including the subdivision of land. Those who wanted less or could only afford smaller tracts found their places as well. All of them worked together to form the foundation of Knightdale.

Panther Rock Plantation, located on today's Hodge Road, was owned by John Hinton and his wife, Grizell Kimbrough. According to the Knightdale Historical Society, Mary Hinton described the home as having no door on the ground floor. Instead, according to the society, a trapdoor was accessed by ladder. This method was meant to keep out undesirables. The plantation was named for the rock formation seen here. (Authors' collections.)

The Oaks Plantation house, built around 1790, faced west. It was originally owned by David Hinton Sr. and his wife, Jane Lewis Hinton. According to Wayne Schulz of the Knightdale Historical Society, the plantation was the site of a prison in the early 1900s. After renovation, the house now faces east and the property includes a cemetery, where 14 family members are buried. (Authors' collections.)

At the north end of Smithfield Road is the Beaver Dam Plantation House, built by William Hinton in 1810. He, along with his brothers, Charles and David, owned three local plantations. Beaver Dam is the northernmost of the Hinton plantations. Later owned by the Walter Jeffreys family, it was said to be haunted in the mid-1900s after a Jeffreys family member saw a ball of fire float out of the chimney and disappear into a nearby cemetery. In 2005, Charles Silver, a Hinton descendant, bought the plantation. He has preserved it and uses it as an office for Hinton Land, LLC, M. Silver & Company. Silver's plan is to use the plantation home as a historic gathering place. The outbuildings are gone, and the land has been sold to a church and to the developer of a nearby subdivision. The house is intact and provides visitors with a glimpse into the 1800s. (Authors' collections.)

David Stone, governor of North Carolina from 1808 to 1810, is buried on Hodge Road near his Restdale Plantation. According to the Knightdale Historical Society, Stone went on to be a US senator. He developed a reputation as an independent, refusing to vote along party lines. He was censured in 1814 and resigned. Stone died in 1818. His tombstone was finally placed in 1984. (Authors' collections.)

Located across Knightdale Boulevard from Green Pines subdivision, this marker is the only reminder that Clay Hill Plantation existed. The plantation belonged to John Hinton and his wife, Pherebee. Hinton, an early settler of the area, fought to end British rule and became a major in the militia of Wake County. (Authors' collections.)

Though it was moved to make way for the Shoppes at Midway, Midway Plantation stayed on Hinton land. According to the plantation website, the move included a journey through Wake Stone property and on narrow two-lane roads. The Hinton descendants say that the three-mile trip was worth the effort, allowing them to restore the plantation buildings originally owned by Charles Hinton. The kitchen and well house were kept separate, for safety. Kitchens often had fires, and water was needed to fight them. The move took place in 2005, and included all of the buildings of the plantation—the house and four outbuildings. The 1848 home withstood a move through a rock quarry site and curvy country roads. This photograph was taken after the house was restored at its new location. The land on which it now stands is on Old Crews Road and was part of the original Hinton plantations. (Authors' collections.)

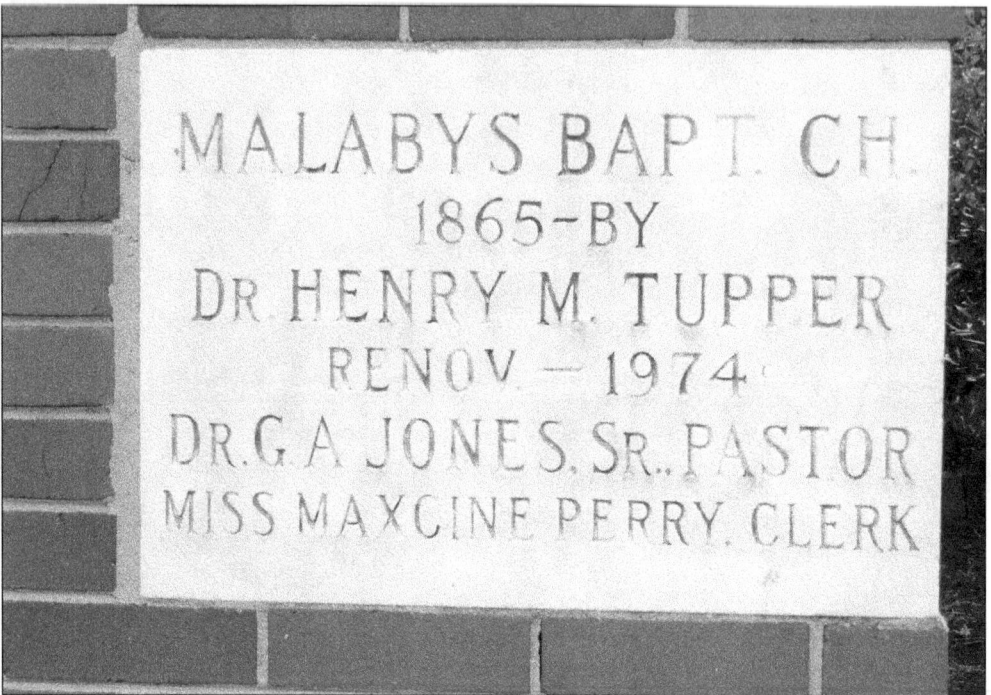

Malaby's Baptist Church, an African American church, was organized in 1865. Today, it is known as Malaby's Crossroads Baptist Church, a name that fits on few cornerstones. The land came from John Hinton's plantation and is shown in his will, in Book 14, page 367 for Wake County Superior Court as given "for the use of all Christian Clergymen to preach on and for the benefit of the community to be used solely as a place for divine worship." This provision applies to all subsequent owners and is noted in the 1976 title granted to the church. The building is now used by a Hispanic congregation, Ministerio Cristo La Solucion. (Both, authors' collections.)

Malaby's Crossroads Baptist Church was established at the end of the Civil War. In the late 1900s, the congregation's growth created the need to move, as the church had only one acre of land on Smithfield Road. The newly widened road had taken part of that acre. A new church building now occupies a site at 911 Old Knight Road and provides the opportunity for congregational growth. (Authors' collections.)

Lockhart School began as an African American school for all grades. With integration, the student body increased, and it became a middle school. Now Lockhart Elementary School, it serves children from kindergarten through fifth grade. Again, because of growth, the school is a year-round institution operating on four tracks. (Courtesy of Knightdale Historical Society.)

Wake Stone Corporation has been a vital part of the town since 1970. It opened on farmland that it purchased in 1970. The site was next to a quarry that had been abandoned a few years earlier. Believing that they could succeed, owner John Bratton and his sons Sam, Ted, and Johnny solicited customer loyalty, and got it. In turn, Wake Stone contributed to the town. Local residents have become employees, and dump truck businesses can operate much more efficiently. Since its founding, Wake Stone has supported the town by furnishing fire trucks, ambulances, and other necessities when need exceeded available money. The Brattons' corporate citizenship has been a model for other companies. The company's headquarters, pictured here, is incorporated into the architectural fabric of the town, just as the Brattons have become interwoven with the life of the community. (Authors' collections.)

Knightdale was once a town with only one doctor, who had a small office and made house calls over a wide area. Now, the town boasts Duke Urgent Care (above), Rex Healthcare (below), and other institutions. Duke provides emergency care, and Rex includes a wellness center. Knightdale is the rare mix of a small town with city services—one more step in becoming a self-sufficient community. (Both, authors' collections.)

Planter's Walk is the town's first planned urban development. It includes retail space at the front, single-family homes, town houses, and recreational facilities. This land was part of Clay Hill and Midway, two of the Hinton plantations. One of the plantation homes is used as the Planter's Walk business office. (Authors' collections.)

The Shoppes of Midway is situated where the now relocated Midway Plantation stood at the town's beginning. The chamber of commerce has long held a goal that residents should be able to live, shop, and work in Knightdale. While it was not the first new shopping area, the Shoppes gathered retail space, medical offices, and restaurants in one area. (Authors' collections.)

Two

MOVING IN AND STARTING ANEW

Life began anew for the area that was to become a town carved from heavy woodland and fertile soil. Hearty pioneers sought a better life for their families. Hard physical labor was a way of life. The railroad brought unprecedented changes to North Carolina. Income drastically changed, as marketing and receiving goods was made easier. Men with vision and entrepreneurial spirit could fully incorporate their ideas for the first time.

Moving to a new area meant transporting all family possessions, in many cases including cows, mules, horses, dogs, cats, and even chickens. As families moved in, they brought their cultural practices with them. These activities were in turn altered by new practices, as residents married into families from other places and cultures.

Peter Knight, father of Henry Haywood Knight, inherited land from his father and used wooden pegs to build this home on a dirt path that is now Old Knight Road. A successful farmer, he raised a family of seven or eight children, as reports vary. The house has been remodeled, and the fireplace from the separate kitchen still stands. (Authors' collections.)

John Lee Weathers (second from left) stands with his wife in front of the fence at their early-1900s home. Next are, from left to right, Rupert Ryan and Haywood Weathers. Tenant farmers who lived on the property are pictured behind the fence. This photograph offers a glimpse of life as it had been for generations, including horses and typical work clothing, and life as it would become, with automobiles and more stylish clothing. (Authors' collections.)

20

Henry Haywood Knight, son of Peter Knight, grew up on the family farm on today's Old Knight Road. He left home to serve in the Confederate army. At the end of the war, Knight was a prisoner at Fort Delaware. He and other prisoners were daily marched to an open area and given the opportunity to swear allegiance to the Union. Doing so would have allowed Knight to return home. Each day, he refused. Finally, Knight and the other remaining prisoners were told to return home. He married Bettie Rufus Smith, with whom he fathered six children. Seeing the need for better access to more communities, Knight approached the Raleigh & Pamlico Sound Railroad Company about building a depot in the area. He and Needham Jones sold right-of-way to the company, which was bought by Norfolk & Southern Railroad soon after. The town adopted the name of Knightdale in his honor. (Courtesy of Nancy Hargrove.)

Bettie Rufus Smith, daughter of Rufus Acral Smith, married Henry Haywood Knight on May 2, 1894. In addition to soliciting the railroad station, they were instrumental in developing a school on their land. Their property included much of the land from the Neuse River to the Knight home on Tarborough Road. The next farm belonged to her brother Acral. Knight's Chapel Church was also on their land. Later, the church moved into Knightdale and changed its name to Knightdale Baptist Church. Bettie's children include Cassie, Mary Elizabeth, Rachel, Henry, and Lucy. After her husband's death on May 7, 1904, she married Rev. Joseph Hilliard. They had one daughter, Ruth. Bettie's niece, Claris Smith Jones, described her aunt as no pushover, but a kind person. By all accounts, that independence was a trait among the Smith women. Maybe it was required in order to thrive in a late-1800s and early-1900s world. (Courtesy of Nancy Hargrove.)

Henry Haywood and Bettie Smith Knight lived in this home on Tarborough Road. The house has undergone many address changes without moving from its original location. Tarborough Road, Highway 64, and Knightdale Boulevard are among the changing road names. The accompanying tenant house was adapted to other uses when tenant farming ceased. The residence has had many alterations, including modernization of the kitchen and an added upstairs porch on the back. In the 1950s, Rachel Horton, the Knights' daughter, used both an electric stove and a woodstove in the kitchen. In the 1980s, Nancy Hargrove, Henry and Bettie's granddaughter, applied for and received recognition in the National Register of Historic Places, which limits some alterations but also preserves an important part of local history. The home, which remains in the family, is the residence of Henry and Bettie Knight's great-grandson, Stephen Hargrove. (Authors' collections.)

Henry Haywood Knight and Bettie Knight Hilliard are buried, along with other Knight ancestors and descendants, in the Knight cemetery on Old Knight Road, across from the house that Knight's father built. That home, erected with wooden pegs, is still in use today. Several generations before, the Knight family came to the area from Chatham County. (Authors' collections.)

Gins made processing cotton easier, faster, and more profitable. Knight Gin in Knightdale, was on the southeast corner of Smithfield and Tarborough Roads, now Knightdale Boulevard. Later, Knightdale Gin was on First Avenue, near the railroad. In this photograph, Acral Smith (left) and George Harris stand in the yard of the first Knight Gin. (Authors' collections.)

The Knightdale Gin was across from today's Knightdale Tractor on Bethlehem Church Road. Farmers could have their cotton cleaned and baled for market. Though it had a variety of owners over the years, the gin was last operated by Audie Faison and his son Roderick "Tink" Faison. It was torn down in the late 1950s. (Courtesy of Peggy Andrews.)

This saw is an example of those used at early sawmills. Only very experienced woodsmen would dare linger near this saw while in operation. The reason for workers losing fingers or whole hands is clear, considering the size of the teeth and the lack of safety guards. This saw was considered an improvement over earlier versions. (Courtesy of Gary McConkey.)

Logging was more hazardous in the 1940s. This photograph shows a large truck hauling a logging cart to the woods. With its multiple long horns, spotlight, and four mirrors, the truck is a stark contrast to today's vehicles. Log carts were pulled out of the woods by horses and mules. The huge logs were possible because the soil promoted pine tree growth. (Courtesy of Gary McConkey.)

The Knights were quite entrepreneurial. They farmed, ran a country store that carried everything from food to coffins, and owned a cotton gin and a sawmill. The sawmill employees shown here are, from left to right, Eli Hinton, Tom Hester, Acral Smith, Jim Harris, Louis Rogers, Scott Wilson, and George Rogers. The sawmill looks like a confusing place to modern eyes. Located across the road from the Smith residence, the mill featured a steam-powered saw, a step up from sawing by hand. Electric saws came into use considerably later. The mill appears to have had additions built as they were needed, a seemingly sensible practice still in use. Note the Barnum & Bailey Circus posters. The likely compensation for use of the side of the building would have been tickets to the circus. (Authors' collections.)

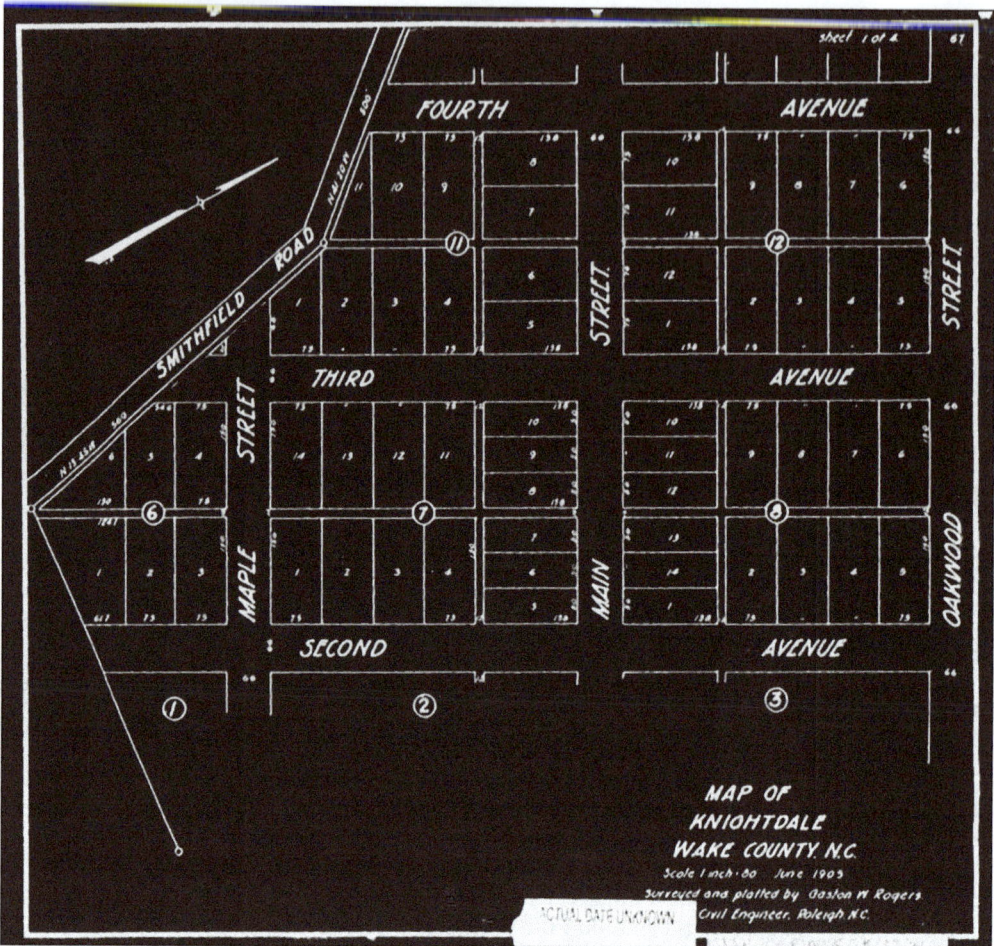

MAP OF
KNIGHTDALE
WAKE COUNTY. N.C.
Scale 1 inch = 80   June 1905
Surveyed and platted by Gaston W Rogers
Civil Engineer, Raleigh. N.C.

In June 1905, Gaston W. Rogers surveyed the town, dividing it into lots and streets, at the request of Bettie Smith Knight. Note that the lots are 150 feet deep, with most being 50 feet wide. Some are 76 feet wide. Small lots were quite common at that time. The development of the railroad provided access to other places, but local transportation was still limited to the horse and buggy. Few people had cars. Small lots allowed more people to live near necessary services. Though stores carried a variety of merchandise, citizens would need to be able to access that merchandise without having to walk too far. Small lots were more affordable, as well. This layout was the beginning of economic development as it is known today. It is a return to smaller lots and mixed-use living. (Courtesy of Register of Deeds.)

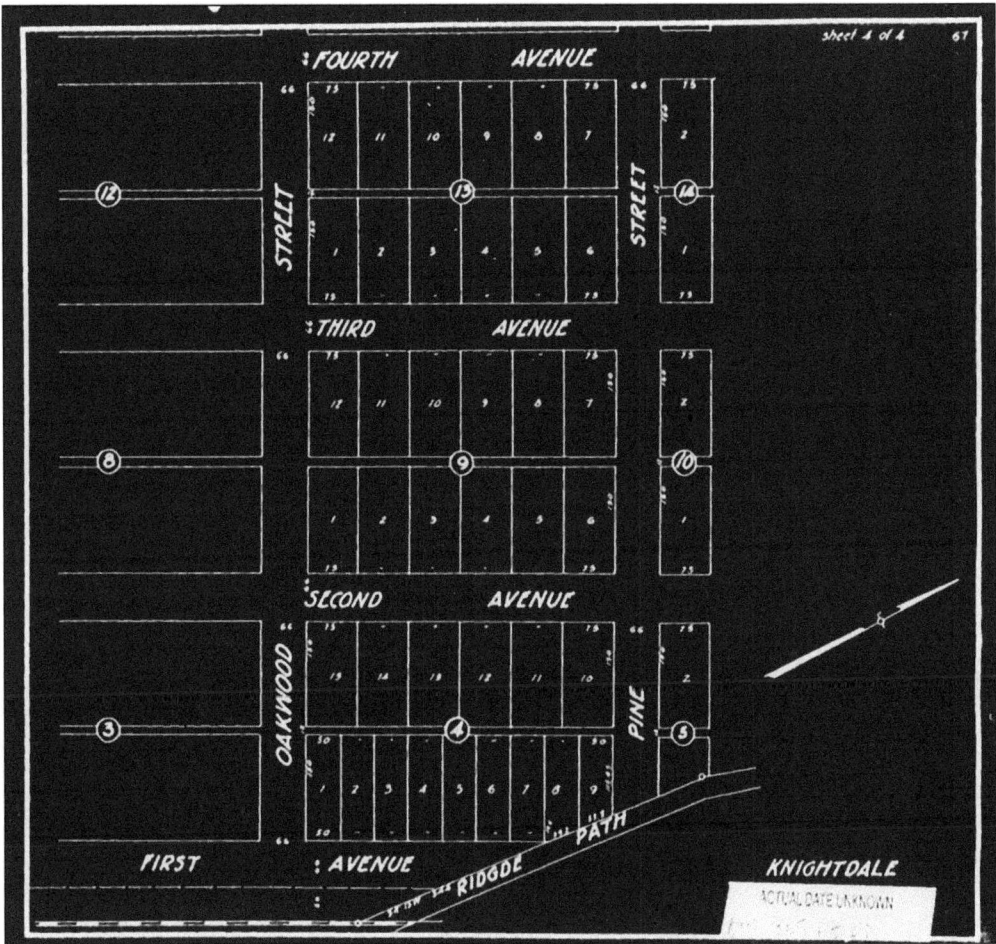

With its lots surveyed and its streets laid out, Knightdale possessed a greater sense of reality in the minds of its citizens as well as on paper. Suddenly, the town had named streets, though some of them were never opened. Fifth Avenue, not shown here, is an example of a street that did not become a reality, because the property owner did not develop that land. The 12-foot service alleys were included because the area near the railroad was planned for commercial use. Ridge Path did not develop at the angle shown here, so refinements were made as needed. Ridge Street, however, does exist as a one-block street running parallel to the elementary school. Such forward-thinking helped development and established the vision and spirit that exists today. In the 1980s, the remaining alleys were closed, because most commercial use shifted to Knightdale Boulevard. (Courtesy of Register of Deeds.)

A section foreman's house was built in 1905, because the foreman had to be readily available. Railroad workers inspected their section of track for damage, out-of-place rails, and the proper amount of ballast stone between the rails to prevent fire. Erastus Cain, Solomon Harrell, and Arthur King were the only foremen to occupy the house. Upon King's retirement, the railroad released the house to him. (Courtesy of John Stalvey.)

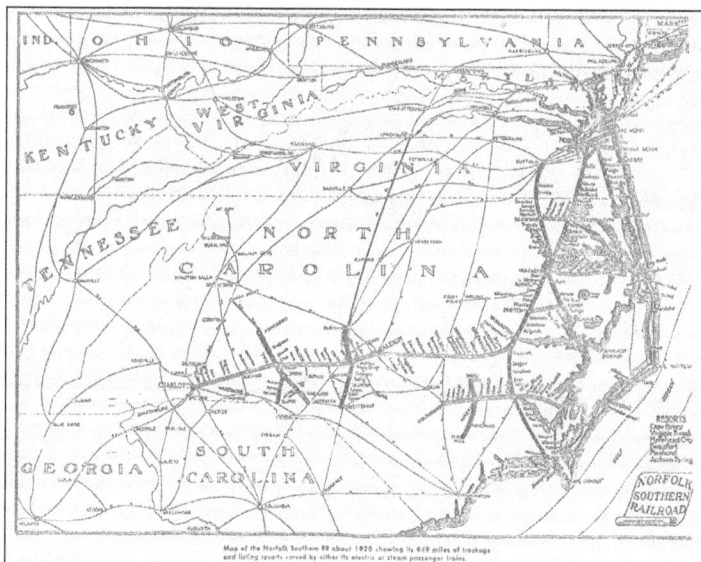

Of 949 miles of Norfolk Southern track, the steepest part was the grade just west of town. When trains were traveling east, the engineer would separate the cars into two sections using the sidetrack at Knightdale, pull the first half to the top of the grade, and go back for the second half. Despite this inconvenience, the train was a huge improvement in moving people and commodities. (Courtesy of Sam Maise.)

Three

NO MORE SNAKE OIL

The town saw unimaginable changes, all of which excited the few citizens of Knightdale. Having readily available medical services was wonderful and new to them. Mothers allowed themselves to hope that the infant death rate would drop. Families were larger; prior to this time, many children died in infancy.

Knightdale became a center of local activity, with mail services, stores, and a pharmacy. Sunday was church day. Saturday brought mules, wagons, and buggies to town. While in town, area residents could trade eggs for sugar or buy a few essentials for the coming week. In the general store, men swapped stories, played a little Rook or checkers, and chewed a little—or a lot of—tobacco. Women went to the store, usually in search of cloth for sewing, new shoes, or household staples such as salt, pepper, and flour.

Needham Jones and his wife, Meto, lived in a home that still stands on Smithfield Road. Along with the Knights, they conveyed right-of-way to the Raleigh & Pamlico Sound Railroad Company for $1, as was the custom when land donations were made. In a statement released immediately following the deed signatures, Justice of the Peace Scarboro states, "E. Meto Jones, the wife of N.P. Jones being by me privately examined, separate and apart from her said husband, touching her voluntary consent to the execution of the said deed, states upon such examination that she executed the said deed voluntarily of her own free will and accord, without any force, fear or undue influence upon the part of her said husband or any other person, and that she does still voluntarily consent to the execution thereof." If she had opposed it, would she have been willing to say so? (Authors' collections.)

Nymphus House built the first brick store in Knightdale at First Avenue and Main Street. The store was named N.G. House & Brothers in 1920, House Union Mercantile in 1921, and, later, N.G. House & Son. The building now houses Stained Glass Associates. (Courtesy of Christine House.)

Shown here are, from left to right, (first row) Ezra and Harper House; (second row) Needham and Nymphus House. The brothers were cousins of James Rufus House. James Rufus and his wife, Bettie Saintsing House, were the parents of Bertha, Eunice Eddie, and Ethel House. (Courtesy of Christine House.)

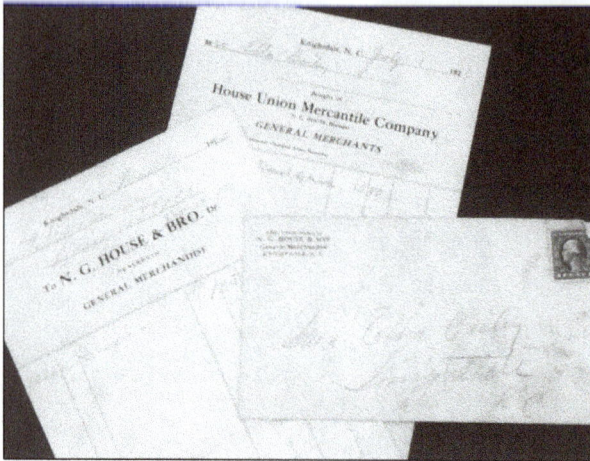

Ella Bailey's March 1, 1920, receipt for shingles is a welcome sight compared to today's prices. In addition, an envelope includes only the addressee's name, city, and state. Even in the mid-1990s, Knightdale postal carriers knew customers so well that such incomplete information was enough. All three incarnations of the House business name are represented—N.G. House & Son, N.G. House & Brothers, and House Union Mercantile. (Courtesy of Mary Jo Cashion.)

The building that initially contained N.G. House is now home to 55-year-old Stained Glass Associates. The company is world renowned for its stained-glass expertise. This photograph shows 100-year-old church windows undergoing restoration. Skilled craftsmen have carefully produced windows for Knightdale Baptist Church, Bethlehem Baptist Church, and many others. (Authors' collections.)

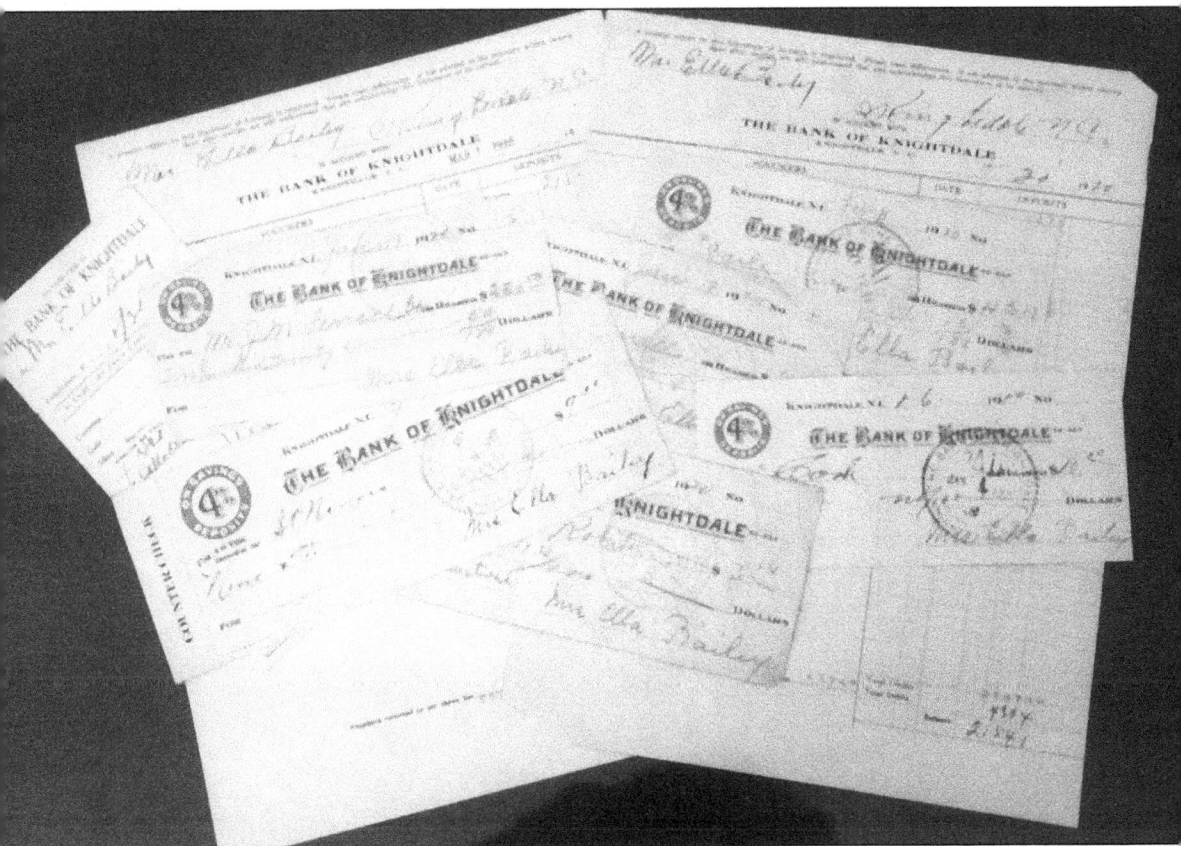

Shown here are documents related to Ella Bailey's account with the Bank of Knightdale. The bank began during Dr. Joseph Hester's tenure in Knightdale and closed in the 1920s. At the time, records were kept by hand at banks and other businesses. The deposit slip on the left distinguishes among gold, silver, and currency, as well as checks. (Courtesy of Mary Jo Cashion.)

Otelia House Ferrell was the wife of Walter A. Ferrell. Their children were Birdie Lee, Myrtle, Virginia, and Mary Elizabeth. Walter and his brothers Raymond and Ivan built much of the new construction in the area. Building became a good way to make a living as the area grew. With ample timber and people in need of housing, Knightdale continued on its path to prosperity. (Courtesy of Christine House.)

Artist and Knightdale native Peggy Andrews provides a glimpse into the town before the 1940 fire. The covered walks and variety of small stores provided places to shop and visit. Note the 25¢ haircuts, 10¢ fatback, and 15¢-per-gallon gas. The gas prices look great, but the era's incomes must be taken into consideration. (Courtesy of Peggy Andrews.)

Dr. Joseph Robert Hester (1881–1965) was the first town doctor. Born in Franklin County, he was one of nine children of William Henry and Louie Virginia Goswick Hester. When he was a boy, his family moved to the Wendell area. Hester studied at the University of North Carolina and taught school briefly before returning to the university in 1906 to attend medical school. He graduated in 1910 as a member of the last graduating class when the medical school was in Raleigh, and he started his medical practice in Knightdale. Hester lived and practiced medicine in town from 1910 to 1929. He was very active in the life of the community. In addition to making house calls throughout the area, he maintained an office across a dirt path from the side of his home. (Courtesy of Mary Jo Cashion.)

The home of Dr. Joseph Hester and his wife, Susie, is still in use on First Avenue. The Sears Modern Home was one of the first delivered to Knightdale by train. It was built shortly after the Hesters married in 1911. Over the years, owners have made additions, such as a side porch, garage, and underpinning. At the time it was built, homes were generally left open underneath, and the home itself rested on pillars of brick or stone. The Hester home was one of several that marked the beginning of the residential section of town. In the early 1900s, homes and businesses were less separated than they are now. As an example, Dr. Hester's office was between two homes. Since the mid-1900s, the structure has been the home of Gene and Doris Anthony. The longevity of the residence speaks to the quality of prefab homes of that era. (Courtesy of Mary Jo Cashion.)

Virginia Frances Hester was the first of eight children born to Knightdale's Joseph and Susie Hester. Virginia was born in 1912 and attended Wendell High School, Mars Hill College, and Meredith College. In 1940, she married Sidney Chamblee Eddins of Zebulon, where she lived until her death in 1995. The couple had one child, Virginia "Ginny" Anne Eddins (1948–2012). (Courtesy of Mary Jo Cashion.)

The first six children of Dr. and Mrs. Joseph Robert Hester were born in their home in Knightdale. Virginia (1912–1995) is standing in the center. The others are, from left to right, Margueritte Hester Price (1921–2008), Susie Nelson Hester Wear (1920–2002), baby Robert Ferguson Hester (1925–), William Henry Hester (1918–1993), and Joseph McMurray "Mack" Hester (1919–2008). After the family moved to Wendell in 1929, two other children were born. (Courtesy of Mary Jo Cashion.)

Dr. Joseph Hester (second from right) owned a drugstore in Knightdale. According to the store letterhead on a note written by Dr. Hester on November 18, 1911, J.R. Hester Drug Company, on First Avenue, offered "drugs, patent medicines, toilet articles, stationery, etc." While in Knightdale, Dr. Hester organized and became vice president of the Bank of Knightdale. In addition, he also served as St. Matthews township chairman of the United War Work and the War Savings Stamps campaigns during World War I. In 1925, he was president of the Wake County Medical Society. Dr. Hester served as chairman of the school board for 10 years, during a time of increasing enrollment in the Knightdale school. The other men in the photograph are not identified. (Courtesy of Mary Jo Cashion.)

Samuel Dolphin Griffin was one of the four large landowners when the town began. This photograph shows him seated with his wife, Delia Bell Griffin. They are surrounded by seven of their ten children. They are, from left to right, (first row) Mozelle, Jack, and Jimmy; (second row) Hallie, Carrie, Alma, and Samuel. Having given birth 10 times, and with all the duties associated with maintaining a home for that many children, Delia's death at 42 is, for the era, not surprising. She died in 1914, and Sam died in 1939. He had remarried and fathered five more children. In addition to farming, Sam operated a large farm supply store at the corner of Tarborough Road and First Avenue. Some of the Griffin land continues to be owned and occupied by the couple's descendants. (Authors' collections.)

Four

REALIZING DREAMS

As more people settled in the area, a time of great vision began in the community. Then, as now, society believed that education was the foundation of a better life. While the men were working to provide for their families, wives and young women focused on better education for everyone. With an innovative pioneering spirit, women overcame the lack of money and provided educational opportunity. Their willingness to work for a common cause was the foundation for generations of education, which continues to enhance the quality of life for the community.

James Ferrell Keith was an active partner in the general merchandise store on First Avenue, known as Robertson & Keith at that time. He and his wife, Lelia Robertson Keith, were very involved in town life. She was the first president of the Women's Betterment Association for Knightdale School, organized in 1912. The membership committee consisted of Rosa Robertson, Eula Ferrell, and Effie Daniels. (Courtesy of Doris Anthony.)

The Robertson house was the only one among the Robertson brothers' homes that survived the 1940 fire. Built by David Jutson "Jut" Robertson, it was only 250 feet from his store, which the fire destroyed. The home was built as a one-story structure, but it was enlarged to two stories in the 1930s. (Courtesy of Dr. Wayne Harper.)

Wiley and Rosa Robertson pose on their wedding day. An entrepreneur, Wiley farmed, delivered the mail in Wendell, built many houses, and owned the drugstore building. During the winter, he butchered and sold meat from the trunk of his car, a normal distribution system for that time. Robertson's favorite pastime was eating at Bob Melton's Barbecue in Rocky Mount. He was a soft touch for a Coke, especially if his grandson Bobby Harrell asked. Rosa chaired the 1912 membership committee of the Betterment Association and was very active in community life. She was an integral part of helping bring hot lunches to Knightdale School and working for other Betterment projects, such as the purchase of a piano for the school. Later in her life, she worked in the drugstore. (Courtesy of Doris Anthony.)

The Women's Betterment Association for Knightdale School was the forerunner of today's Home Extension Homemakers Club. The group first met on March 1, 1912, when the school was on the Knight farm. The three-room building on First Avenue opened in 1914, and the association raised and sold cotton to bring in money for school needs. In 1915, it purchased a piano for the school for over $300, paying for it incrementally. The association also raised the money required to dig the well for school use. The members seem to have maintained their senses of humor, as seen in the above photograph's arrangement of hoes. Note that even the children were involved. Below, the association members get ready to enjoy a welcome drink of water from the well. (Both, courtesy of Mary Jo Cashion.)

Knightdale's first town school was a three-room structure built about 1914 between the cemetery and the original Knightdale Methodist Church. These lunch ladies, as they were called then, were made possible by the Betterment Association about 1918. Cooking the 3¢ lunches must have been a hot job. Those hot lunches were the first served in a rural Wake County school. (Courtesy of Mary Jo Cashion.)

Pictured here in her later years, Ella Ferguson Bailey was the 1918 president of the Betterment Association. She and the teachers oversaw the planting of cotton; association members chopped the cotton until school opened; and the students finished the job. Bailey also tried to organize a Boy Scout troop, but that dream did not materialize during her lifetime. (Courtesy of Mary Jo Cashion.)

The relationship among these people is not known, but this may be a group of friends or a Sunday school class. The girl on the far right in the first row is Ginny Hester, daughter of Dr. Joseph Hester and his wife, Susie. (Courtesy of Mary Jo Cashion.)

PEGGY JANELLE ANDREWS

The Jake Andrews house stood where Knightdale Medical Center and Community Helpers Service do today. On Saturday afternoons, area men would gather in the yard to play marbles. The marble ring is depicted in the lower right corner of the drawing. While people rarely play marbles today, the game was a mainstay of fellowship and relaxation in the 1920s and 1930s. (Courtesy of Peggy Andrews.)

In about 1914, Knightdale School opened between the cemetery and the original United Methodist church. With the growing number of children in town, the school's new location was ideal. It had previously operated on the Henry Knight farm. This school was the first in Wake County to have hot lunches, thanks to the Betterment Association. The spirit of volunteering carried through the work of the society, as it purchased a piano and other needed items for the students. Surely, today's local Parent-Teacher Associations evolved from this early involvement in Knightdale and other communities. (Courtesy of Peggy Andrews.)

While the building still exists in a separate location, this rendering of the train depot provides a glimpse into the town's early years. Moving goods and people was the basis of the town's burgeoning existence. Until the railroad came, products could not be sufficiently shipped to make a profit. In addition, supplies often could not meet demand before the railroad. (Courtesy of Peggy Andrews.)

Wiley and Claude Robertson's houses are in the background of this photograph of their father, George Robertson, and his early-20th-century automobile, possibly a Stanley. Note the steering wheel on the right side, despite his sitting on the left side. Robertson was quite a dashing figure as he drove down First Avenue. (Courtesy of Doris Anthony.)

Jutson and Hattie Robertson stand beside a local house. The expression on Hattie's face may mean that Jutson is in trouble, or that she is amused by something she sees or by something he said. Jutson Robertson was a great lover of life. He fished and ran a store. His preference, of course, was fishing. (Courtesy of Dr. Wayne Harper.)

Knightdale Baptist Church grew out of Knight's Chapel Baptist Church, located west of the Henry Haywood Knight house on Tarborough Road, today's Knightdale Boulevard. It was organized on March 17, 1901, with 12 charter members. Rev. C.E. Gower conducted worship service in Knight's School. In 1906, the congregation erected and moved to this building on Main Street. The name change occurred in October 1930. (Courtesy of Knightdale Historical Society.)

This aerial photograph shows the town after the fire of 1940. Evidence of progress includes businesses rebuilt, the Robertson house next to the store (center) that seems to be occupied, a water service in place, and life having resumed. (Courtesy of Gary McConkey.)

Five

Hopes, Dreams, and Smoke

An act of the North Carolina Legislature allowed Knightdale to become an incorporated town. No longer just a community, it had legal standing in the state. The town began to bustle with activity. With a mayor, a constable, and a homegrown doctor, all seemed well. Businesses grew, and more people moved into the area. The depot was busy with people, mail, and the shipping and receiving of goods.

Although everyone knew the potential devastation of fires, no one envisioned most of the downtown businesses going up in flames—certainly not in the new town. However, business district buildings and several houses did burn, and residents were helpless to stop the fire. Churches, strong faith, and perseverance provided the strength the citizens needed to endure this catastrophic time in the life of the town.

A Bill to be Entitled

AN ACT TO INCORPORATE THE TOWN OF KNIGHTDALE.

THE GENERAL ASSEMBLY OF NORTH CAROLINA DO ENACT:

Section 1. That the town of Knightdale in the County

of Wake be and the same is hereby incorporated by the name and

style of " Knightdale," and it shall be governed by and sub-

ject to all provisions of law now existing in reference to

incorporated towns and not inconsistent with this act.

Section 2. That the boundaries of said town of

Knightdale shall be determined as follows:

    Beginning at the South-east corner of the Knightdale
School property, on Fayetteville Street, and runs N.6deg. 45
min. E.4000 feet to the North-east corner of S.A.Watson's lot
on Griffin Street; thence N.74 deg. 45 min. W. 1450 feet to
a point in Mrs.Bettie Hillard's land; thence S.23 deg.W. 2600
feet with Fourth Avenue to the Smithfield Road; thence S.10
deg.W.1000 feet to the North-west corner of the Dillon Gin
property; thence S.30 deg. E. 2210 feet to a point,W.O.Johnson's
land; thence N.59 deg 55 min. E. 1250 feet to the beginning.

Section 3. That the officers of said town shall be

a mayor, treasurer, constable and five aldermen.

Section 4. That B.L.Wall shall be mayor of said town

and N.G.House, J.F.Keith, L.A.Doub, J.T.Ramsey and C.L.Robertson

shall be aldermen and are hereby appointed lawful officers of

Filed by E.D. Flowers, Esquire, the incorporation papers are titled "An Act to Incorporate the Town of Knightdale." The act says that the town will have a mayor, board of aldermen, treasurer, and constable, and that the latter two will be named by the mayor and aldermen. The land survey text is shown here. Bettie Hilliard is the former Bettie Knight. Henry Haywood Knight died before the railroad had time to build tracks through Knightdale. Bettie married Josiah Hilliard and continued the work that she and her first husband had begun. The aldermen included N.G. House, J.F. Keith, L.A. Doub, and C.L. Robertson. Handwritten across the top is "A Bill to Be Entitled." In today's computer age, handwriting on a legal document is uncommon. (Courtesy of North Carolina Archives.)

said town. The treasurer and constable shall be elected by the mayor and board of aldermen. The officers hereby appointed shall hold office until their successors shall be elected in an election to be held in said town on the second Tuesday in May, one thousand nine hundred and twenty eight, and every two years thereafter when the qualified voters of said town shall elect a mayor and five aldermen who shall qualify and take office on the first monday in June next succeeding their election.

Section 5. That the officers appointed in this act shall qualify, within ten days from its ratification, before a Justice of the Peace or Clerk of the Superior Court, and the officers thereafter elected or appointed shall qualify before the Mayor of said town or a Justice of the Peace of Wake County.

Section 6. That said mayor and aldermen shall make such rules, ordinances, regulations and laws as may be necessary for proper government of said town and shall have and may exercise all such rights and authority as are allowed incorporated towns under the general law.

Section 7. That all laws and clauses of laws in conflict with this act are hereby repealed.

Section 8. That this act shall be in force from and after its ratification.

Ratified this the ..... day of ............A.D. 1927.

The ratification on the back (not shown) indicates that it passed three readings on February 26, March 7, and March 8, with unanimous approval and ratification on March 9, 1927. An act of incorporation serves to give a town its own identity. The residents in 1927 never could have realized how important that identity would be in 60 years. Without it, a nearby city or town could grow enough to annex the town. Incorporation makes handling territory disputes easier. Territory disputes are becoming more prevalent because of the financial gain for incorporated areas when they annex nearby land. Towns need revenue to survive, and losing territory is costly. In North Carolina, small, unincorporated towns can easily be absorbed into larger towns and cities. Businesses want to develop an identity that includes place, so they want the safety of incorporated areas as well. (Courtesy of North Carolina Archives.)

As indicated in the incorporation papers, Bennett Lewis Wall was the town's first mayor (1927–1934). A native of Shotwell, he attended Frog Pond Academy. According to Wayne Schulz of the Knightdale Historical Society, prior to earning his living in Knightdale, Wall was a salesman for the New England Insurance Company. He operated Knightdale Drug Company and was postmaster for 27 years—the post office was located in the drugstore. Wall married Evie David Harrison, and they had six children—Elizebeth, Bennett Harrison, Lewis McGinnis, Joyce, Harold, and Ada Burton. He later married Myrtle Umstead, and they had one child, Gail. Wall died in March 1941. He is remembered for his political leadership in securing the paving of First Avenue and Smithfield Road. Such a legacy seems insignificant today, but the transformation of streets from dust and mud to pavement was a tremendous achievement. (Courtesy of Town of Knightdale.)

Along with his involvement in town government, Grover Cleveland Purkerson owned G.C. Purkerson's Grocery in Knightdale. Shown here are his ledger entries for Reuben Wilder's purchases. Reading it appears that it may have been as troublesome as writing all of the information by hand. (Authors' collections.)

David Jutson "Jut" Robertson was a general merchant. A great lover of fishing, he built a small lake on his farm beside Fayetteville Street. Robertson is pictured with his wife, Hattie Mae Weathers, and their daughters Lillian (left) and Pearl. When he could no longer drive a car, Jutson drove his garden tractor to the lake to fish. (Courtesy of Dr. Wayne Harper).

The first water service in town was a private system owned by Lemuel Flowers. The first water line was only one half-inch in diameter, so it froze often. Using water for anything was difficult, because the houses between a customer and the well got water first. The town did not have a municipal water system until the 1950s. (Courtesy of John Stalvey.)

Jut and Hattie Robertson (left) stand with Allie and Joseph Ramsey at the Ramsey house, which remains at the corner of Second and First Avenues. They seem to be very interested in events on or beyond the train track across the street. Since Robertson was a merchant and Ramsey was a lumberman, this photograph must have captured them on a Sunday afternoon. The women are sisters. (Courtesy of Dr. Wayne Harper.)

Landon Anderson Doub served as mayor from 1934 to 1938. He received his law degree from a private lawyer, a Dr. Pell. At that time, anyone wanting to be an attorney could work with a judge in an apprentice relationship to earn a law degree after completing college. Doub operated his law office in a small room in his general store on the corner of Fayetteville and Railroad Streets. The custom of the day was to house one business within another. Mail was picked up at the drugstore, where one could also see the doctor. Insurance was sold in general stores, and law was practiced in them as well. In addition to law work and being mayor, Doub served as the last Wake County treasurer and as a member of the Wake County Draft Board during World War II. He was town attorney and mentored Clarence Kirk, who later became town attorney. (Courtesy of Town of Knightdale.)

Townspeople, using bucket brigades and pots and pans, tried to save the business area and residences in the predawn hours of February 7, 1940. The fire began between 1:30 and 2:30 a.m. in Robertson's Store and was not brought under control until after the Raleigh Fire Department tanker arrived at about 4:30 a.m. The tanker had become stuck in the mud on Smithfield Road. As seen here, very little of the business district was left standing. This fire served as the impetus for the town's developing a water system and a fire department, yet money for this project was unavailable. Through perseverance, faith, and hard work, Knightdale developed a municipal water system in 1952 and a volunteer fire department in October 1953. Many volunteer hours went into achieving this goal. (Courtesy of John Bruce Parrish.)

The big chimneys at right are all that remain of the Wiley Robertson home. To the left are the chimneys of Claude Robertson's home. Knightdale Baptist Church still stands in the background. Its bell rang in emergency mode, and the town tried to put out the fire, but much was lost on February 7, 1940. While the fire was devastating, it ultimately brought renewal. Businesses were rebuilt and homes were replaced. Knightdale reemerged as an agricultural, residential, and economic force in eastern Wake County. The work of replacing the buildings kept the spirit of the relatively new town alive. In the photograph, a man stands on a pillar and others move among the rubble to salvage anything of value. (Courtesy of John Bruce Parrish.)

The very means of providing goods and materials to a thriving town offered a view into the town's darkest night. Passengers on the train that pulled in on February 8, 1940, only a few hours after the fire was brought under control, witnessed quite a sight. First Avenue was filled with cars, but no one was moving. Residents stood and looked at the damage while they talked about starting over. Just beyond the few blocks that were burned, farm buildings, fields lying fallow for winter, and woodlands looked just as they had before tragedy struck. With spring, they would flourish again, as would the town. In years to come, the fire became a lasting memory for those who lived through it and interesting history for those born later. All residents could feel proud of the rebuilding and renewal of the town. (Courtesy of John Bruce Parrish.)

John Elliott Davis did not grow up in Knightdale, but he learned a lot about the concerns of its citizens as he served them at Knightdale Drug Company. Davis was a graduate of Page School of Pharmacy. In addition to being a pharmacist, he made fountain syrups and soft drinks. He served as mayor from 1938 to 1940. (Courtesy of Town of Knightdale.)

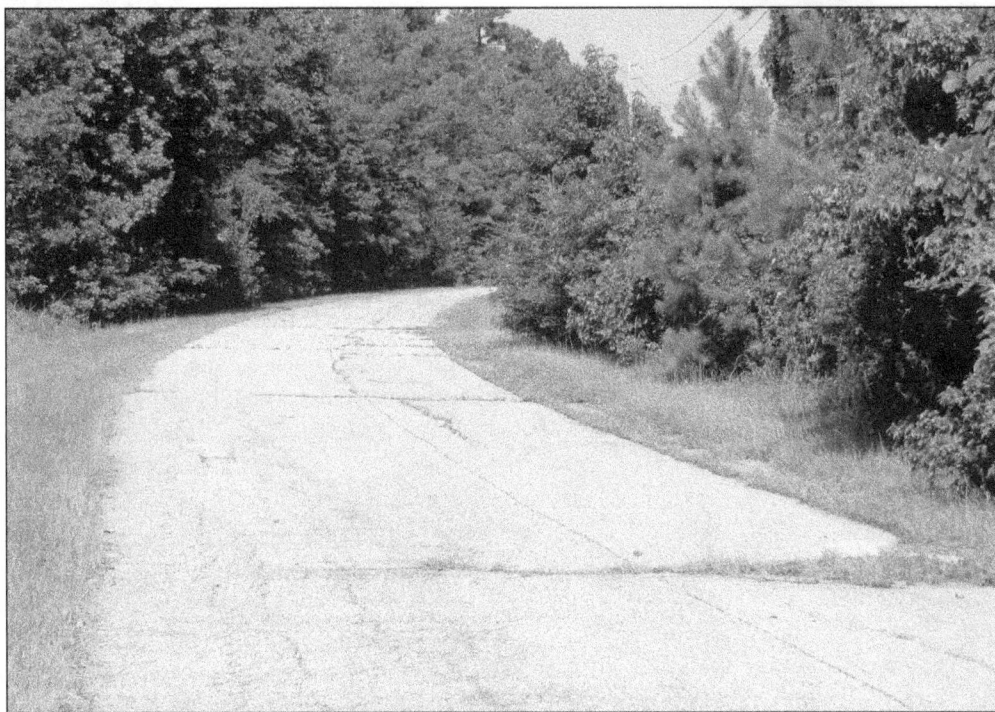

Just west of the Neuse River, this last section of US Route 64 remains from its two-lane days. Prior to 1927, it was a dirt road. Then, an 18-foot-wide slab of concrete was poured. In 1963, the highway became four lanes. This easing of traffic congestion came at a price—a very hot summer, with the front windows of houses closed to avoid the dust. (Authors' collections.)

Oaky Grove Methodist Episcopal Church was the forerunner of today's Knightdale United Methodist Church. It was originally located north of the present site in a grove of oak trees, on land purchased from Bennett Blake. With the 1837 purchase of the current tract of land adjacent to A.T. Mial's property, the church project began. The church shown in the photograph was built around 1876. According to the Knightdale Historical Society, an old church register includes many familiar family names—Debnam, Hodge, Doub, Mial, Blake, Faison, Woodard, Wall, and Lassiter. In July 1917, Knightdale United Methodist was organized, and many Oaky Grove members began attending it. The church history states, "Around 1949, Oaky Grove closed, and the remaining members transferred to Knightdale United Methodist." Oaky Grove sat abandoned for many years. In the late 1990s, restoration began. This photograph reflects that ongoing restoration. (Courtesy of Knightdale Historical Society.)

Knightdale United Methodist Church was organized on July 27, 1917, with Rev. L.E. Sawyer and 10 members. The church history reports that the following people attended the organizational meeting: Mr. and Mrs. A.R. Hodge, Mr. and Mrs. L.L. Allen, Mrs. N.G. House, Mrs. Jeanette Lewis, Richard Hodge, Lucile Allen, L.W. Allen, and L.A. Doub. Members constructed a frame building, which served the congregation until 1948. The first Knightdale Methodist Church was built on First Avenue about 1917 and served the congregation until 1949, when it moved into a larger structure on the same site. Oaky Grove Methodist Episcopal Church at Shotwell closed, and members became part of the newly formed Knightdale Methodist. The building partially visible on the left side of the above photograph is the parsonage, but it became additional church space as needed. Most recently, it has been a fellowship hall. (Both, courtesy of Knightdale Historical Society.)

Dr. Rupert Weathers (left) was the town doctor from October 1926 until June 1958. His offices were in the pharmacy and his home. Weathers often accepted food or goods as payment and claimed to have delivered over 1,200 babies during the years he practiced medicine. He is pictured with two very successful community farmers, Lee Knott (center) and Royal "R.B." Hopkins. The men's dapper dress indicates that the photograph may have been taken on a Sunday, possibly during a discussion of community affairs. Weathers was deeply interested in the community and contributed by tackling tasks that others were not available to do or could not do. Weathers holds a lit cigar, but he is reputed to have rarely smoked. Maybe one of those deliveries has occurred. (Authors' collections.)

Six

WHAT HAPPENED TO NORMAL?

World War II brought about shocking change. Even with World War I in the country's recent memory, war on this larger scale was unimaginable. Normal was nowhere to be found. Would the country be attacked? Surely this question was in the minds of the citizens. Those left at home worked hard to support the war effort, and all able-bodied men went off to fight.

Many older men went to work in the shipyards or at other strategic war jobs. Some local women went to other cities to work in offices or factories. In Knightdale, leaders emerged in schools, in stores, as town officials, and in all areas of life. Men, women, and even children took on new duties during this time.

Postal Telegraph

Mackay Radio   *All America Cables*

Commercial Cables   *Canadian Pacific Telegraphs*

THIS IS A FULL RATE TELEGRAM, CABLE-GRAM OR RADIOGRAM UNLESS OTHERWISE INDICATED BY SYMBOL IN THE PREAMBLE OR IN THE ADDRESS OF THE MESSAGE. SYMBOLS DESIGNATING SERVICE SELECTED ARE OUTLINED IN THE COMPANY'S TARIFFS ON HAND AT EACH OFFICE AND ON FILE WITH REGULATORY AUTHORITIES.

Form 1 AG84 77 GOVT 6 EXTRA CHK US DELY OR OL CHGS ==
DX WASHINGTON 20 826P
MR ARTHUR LEE KING=
       KINIGHTDALE NCAR=

1941 DEC 20 PM 9 56

THE NAVY DEPARTMENT DEEPLY REGRETS TO INFORM YOU THAT YOUR SON LEWIS MEYER KING, FIREMAN FIRST CLASS US NAVY IS MISSING FOLLOWING ACTION IN THE PERFORMANCE OF HIS DUTY AND IN THE SERVICE OF HIS COUNTRY X THE DEPARTMENT APPRECIATES YOUR GREAT ANXIETY AND WILL FURNISH YOU FURTHER INFORMATION PROMPTLY WHEN RECEIVED X TO PREVENT POSSIBLE AID TO OUR ENEMIES PLEASE DO NOT DIVULGE THE NAME OF HIS SHIP OR STATION=

      REAR ADMIRAL RANDALL JACOBS CHIEF OF TTHE BUREAU OF NAVIGATION.

US X X.

The telegraph announcing Lewis King missing in action was sent after the attack on Pearl Harbor. He was the first World War II casualty from Knightdale. The telegram was sent 13 days after the attack, due to the difficulty in keeping an accurate count of soldiers at that time. According to the US Navy, over 2,000 Americans were killed in that attack. (Courtesy of Sam Maise.)

US Navy Fireman First Class Lewis King served on the USS *Arizona* and was killed during the attack on Pearl Harbor. King was the son of Arthur King. As with many towns, Knightdale has seen many young men and women go into war. The Blue Star Memorial includes a garden. It grows at the intersection of Main Street and First Avenue, near the site once occupied by the train depot. The small stone on the right honors King. (Both, courtesy of Sam Maise.)

Knightdale School (above) moved to Ridge Street in 1926, with the first class graduating in 1927. It offered 11 grades and consolidated many small, outlying schools, including Shotwell's Frog Pond Academy. When the county added the 12th grade, less space became available. When space ran out, Vaiden Whitley High School was built on Rolesville Road. In 1965, high school students from Knightdale and Wendell moved into the new school. In the fall of 1970, grades five through eight moved to Lockhart School. The nearby teacherage (below) provided housing for Knightdale teachers. Providing housing for teachers was a common practice in the early 1900s. By the 1950s, the teacherage was no longer needed, due to greater availability of affordable housing. It has been converted to apartments. (Both, courtesy of Knightdale Historical Society.)

Eugene and Lillian Harper stand in the yard of their tenant house. They may be on the way to or from church. Eugene later became mayor. The Harpers had three sons—Jutson, Charles, and Wayne. As of early 2014, Jutson and Charles are retired; Charles lives with his wife, Linda, on family land; and Wayne is a doctor in Raleigh. (Courtesy of Dr. Wayne Harper.)

Billy Wilder, about two years old, sits with his best friend, Laddie, in his grandfather's barnyard. Life in a town was quite different then. Wagons, chickens, and outhouses were the norm. An older child would be able to climb trees, run with the dog, gather eggs, and go to the store for a treat—all in the same area. (Authors' collections.)

This branch of the House family includes James Rufus (seated, right) and Bettie House (seated, center) and their children—Anne Wilder House, Eddie House, Bertha Ferrell House, Eunice House. Anne's family lived in the Needham Jones house, about one-tenth of a mile away. (Courtesy of Christine House.)

Thomas Edwin Smith was a member of the Army Air Corps during World War II when he went to serve immediately after his graduation from North Carolina State College. He did not get to use his agricultural education degree. After returning to the United States, he was killed in a crash while moving a plane to another base for decommissioning. (Authors' collections.)

THE KNIGHTDALE KNEWS

Volume I   Knightdale, N. C., June, 1943   Number 1

—Editorials— LETTERS AND MORE LETTERS

Ask the first service man you meet if he were adrift in the Pacific which he would prefer mail from home or water, chances are he would reply "mail".

Take time from your busy day at the office, in the fields, weeding the garden, sewing, driving your car, at your work and write a letter to someone in the service of Uncle Sam.

When the Sergeant calls "John Doe" and "Richard Roe" fails to hear his name in spite of his bravado about not caring there is an empty feeling in the pit of his stomach.

One boy tells of having received a number of letters and of the envious looks which followed him to his bunk. Letters and more letters are the mark of popul... *letters* frozen peaks of ... *and more letters* muddy canal, ... *our boys!* tell of bells, jobs, men... the th... an... inc... ly th... th... ou...

PROPOSED TOWN BUDGET FOR 1943

Street Lights	
Mayor's Salary	$303.96
Tax Collector and Listing	60.00
Hall Rent	200.00
Rent on Garbage Lot	20.00
Police Service	10.00
Street Work	50.00
Sanitation	50.00
	60.00
TOTAL	$753.96

This 21st day of May 1943.
R. R. Weathers, Mayor

H...
Rent...
Police ...
Street Work ...
Sanitation ...

TOTAL $753.96
This 21st day of May 1943.
R. R. Weathers, Mayor

SHALL WE HAVE A NEWSPAPER

Would you like to have a monthly newspaper for Knightdale? Subscription rates to such a paper will be low. Its contents will be mainly local news items. Knightdale citizens who have moved away, and our men in Armed Services of our country are interested in what is going on in Knightdale. Many will welcome such a book... bourn, who has had training in this field can some of her time to ed. ad- paper. It will be a non-terprise, published solely benefit of the community.

Are you interested? To tion of the paper is a trip us know how you feel a monthly newspaper. So write to Mrs. Elizabeth bourn, Mr. John Stalvey, or bricks, at K...

TYPHOID VACCINATION

The annual typhoid vaccination will be given at... store on the ... June ... 14th.

FOOD PRESERVATION COURSE

Mrs. S. A. Watson is preparing to teach a course on "Food Preservation" for the women of this and nearby communities. Leaders from the Broadwell, Bethlehem, Samaria, Shotwell, Bethany, Wilder's Grove and Knightdale will receive instructions in canning, drying and other methods of food preservation. Actual demonstrations are to be held at the classes. Miss Grace Newell, home economics teacher, is organizing the various sections into workable districts so that each home may be instructed in a safe method of preparing fruits and vegetables for winter use.

The Club w... day of ea... cafeteria course in foo... month. Mrs. C. S. McInnis... instruct club members. Mrs. C. A. Sallinger, president, urges all members to be present.

INTERMEDIATE B. T. U. SOCIAL

The Intermediate B. T. U. held its quarterly social at the home of Mrs. Ernest Fulghum, the new leader. Following a number of games a social hour was held. Ice cream and cake was served to 18 members.

SERVICE MEN'S PICTURES IN DRUG STORE

Stalvey has arranged a way of reminding townspeople the many local boys serving Uncle Sam at home and on foreign battle fronts. The drug store hangs snapshots of local... He grateful for contributions as there... our boys who...

SUPPLEMENTARY RATION OF SUGAR

... canning ... rationing ... sugar supply. The following persons volunteered to assist in rationing: Mrs. Bodie Cooley, Mrs. Ed Montague, Mrs. C. E. Wilder, Mrs. William Wilder, Mrs. L. E. Flowers, Mrs. Stanley Dickerson, Mrs. C. A. Sallinger, Mrs. C. H. Hall, Misses Doris Hildebran, and Grace Newell, H. B. Baum, G. A. Hendricks and Mrs. Earl Wilbourn.

Mrs. L. O. King and family of near Garner visited Mrs. G. W. Wall Thursday.

Volume I, no. 1 of the *Knightdale Knews* was published in June 1943. The paper gave local news, which often included helpful information for making less go further, the town budget, rationing, and the latest about the men in the military. The paper ceased publication with the ending of World War II. Elizabeth Wall Wilbourn, daughter of Bennett Wall, was the originator of the paper, and this edition was the trial run. It was published monthly. Her idea was to help everyone through the difficult war years. Many residents had gone to fight or to work in factories or offices, while others were trying to keep life going at home. Rationing was in place, which meant that careful planning was required to stretch food and gas as far as they would go. Supplementary rations of sugar and the availability of ration books were announced. Writing to servicemen and posting their pictures in the drugstore were encouraged. (Courtesy of Sam Maise.)

Postmistress Myrtle Wall occupies herself during a lull in business in the town's second post office. It was in the Knightdale Drug Company, the business of her husband, Bennett Wall, where it had been during the 27 years he spent as postmaster. One-stop shopping was available even then. Customers could collect their mail, get a sweet treat, browse the shelves, and have a prescription filled in the same place. Coca-Cola was 5¢, as was ice cream. It became an information center, much like country stores. Residents could learn news of the day, whether of the community or the greater area. Prior to the existence of a business to host it, the first post office had been in the home of James "Jim" Ferrell. (Courtesy of Knightdale Historical Society.)

DRINK Coca-Cola

HARRELL'S CASH STORE

PEGGY JANELLE ANDREWS

Harrell's store still stands today, next to the church in the Wall Plumbing storefront on Fayetteville Street. As did most small towns, Knightdale had a variety of general stores. Harrell's was a general merchandise store. Located near the railroad and the burgeoning residential community, it was convenient for people who needed flour, sugar, and the like. (Courtesy of Peggy Andrews.)

Born in Cross County, Arkansas, Elijah Daniel Flowers moved with his family to Wilson when he was a small boy. According to the Knightdale Historical Society, he was a graduate of Rock Ridge High School in Wilson County and of Wake Forest Law School. By this time, law schools had been established. Early in his career, Flowers was justice of the peace in Wilson County. He then practiced law in Raleigh and Wake County for many years. Flowers filed the incorporation papers for Knightdale and handled general law for its citizens. His practice required that he be well-versed in all types of law, though much of his practice involved land transactions. Specialization would not lend itself to making a decent living. Living in the Sidney Faison house on Smithfield Road, he served as mayor from 1940 to 1942, continuing to practice law until his death in 1955. (Courtesy of Town of Knightdale.)

This is a 1940s eighth-grade class at Knightdale School. The class's size, 39 students, attests to the growth in the area. Evident in the photograph are the awkwardness, the need to fit in, and the silliness that still accompany adolescence. Those who grew up in Knightdale may find ancestors in this group, or at least people whose family resemblances are so strong that they can be easily associated with their relatives. (Courtesy of Knightdale Historical Society.)

Clay Cooper stands beside his service station at the intersection of Tarborough and Smithfield Roads. He and his wife, Mattie Lee, lived above the station and worked it together. During much of the 20th century, companies would paint businesses without charge in exchange for advertising space. This station is painted with an eye-catching Coca-Cola ad that also bears the station's name. (Courtesy of Knightdale Historical Society.)

Juanita keeps a hand on her son, John T. "Little John" Massey Jr., while posing for the camera at her husband's service station, at the intersection of today's Old Knight Road and Knightdale Boulevard. The station attendant pumped the gas by hand lever into the bowl on top of the pump for measuring. The gas then traveled by hose into the car's tank. (Courtesy of John Massey Jr.)

Seven

DIRT IS NOT DIRTY AND SWEAT IS OK

The basis of the community and town of Knightdale was agriculture. Farmers and loggers provided the business for stores, which in turn provided the goods needed to till the soil and the necessary clothing for families. Days on the farm were long and difficult, often lasting 12, even 14 hours in the summer. The ability to perform demanding physical work earned the utmost respect. Farmers prepared their land, planted and tilled the crops, and hoped for a good payday in the fall. Some paydays were good, while some were bleak. The uninitiated would expect winter to be a time of rest, but it brought extra work, keeping the fireplaces and cookstoves supplied with wood. For the mother and girls of the family, Monday was wash day, no matter what the season, with washpots to boil and clothes to scrub.

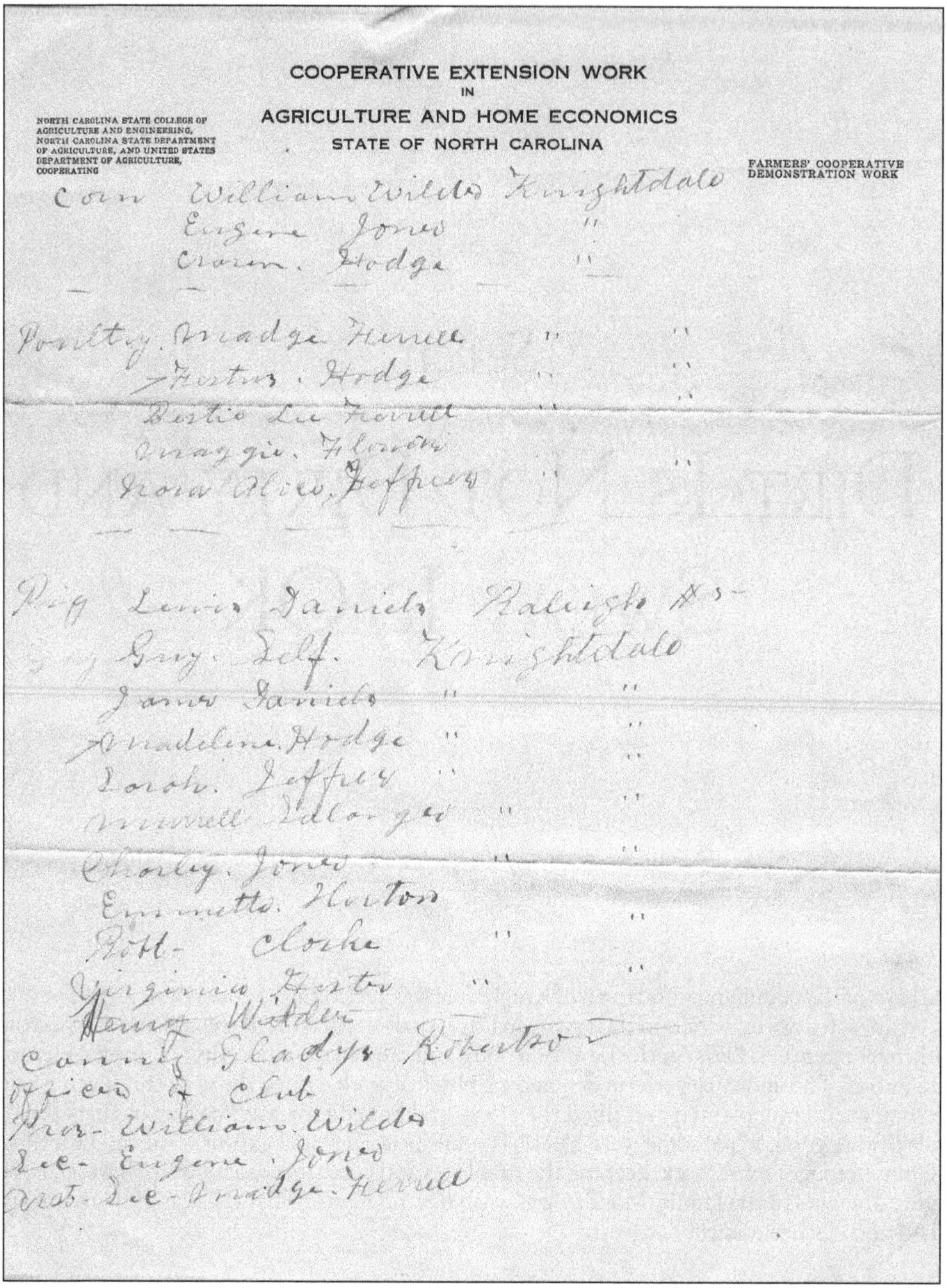

NORTH CAROLINA STATE COLLEGE OF
AGRICULTURE AND ENGINEERING,
NORTH CAROLINA STATE DEPARTMENT
OF AGRICULTURE, AND UNITED STATES
DEPARTMENT OF AGRICULTURE,
COOPERATING

FARMERS' COOPERATIVE
DEMONSTRATION WORK

(handwritten list)

Corn — William Wilds — Knightdale
Eugene Jones — "
Crowen Hodge — "

Poultry — Madge Ferrell —
Hester Hodge —
Bertie Lee Ferrell
Maggie Flowers
Nora Alice Jeffers

Pig — Lewis Daniels — Raleigh #5
Guy Self — Knightdale
James Daniels — "
Madeline Hodge — "
Sarah Jeffers — "
Maxwell Salenger — "
Charley Jones —
Emmett Horton —
Robt Clarke — "
Virginia Horton —
Henry Widder —
Canning — Gladys Robertson
Officers of club
Pres — William Wilds
Sec — Eugene Jones
Vice Pres — Madge Ferrell

This 1920 list of people participating in the North Carolina State Fair and organizing the local agriculture club shows interest in improving farm practices. The local club was the suggestion of Wake County extension agent W.H. Chamblee. He suggested to Ella Bailey that free fair passes might be possible for participants. Chamblee is believed to have lived in the Wakefield area, just outside of Zebulon. Surely, he would have had a special interest in involving the eastern side of the county, since he lived there. He also probably saw the advantages to farmers meeting and exchanging ideas. That spirit of learning still exists through the extension service offered by North Carolina State University and through each county's extension service. Those with ancestors in the Knightdale area are likely to find a relative on the list. (Courtesy of Gary McConkey.)

Woodsheds provided places to store dry wood. This shed at Henry Rufus Knight's house stored wood for cooking, heating, making tobacco sticks, and many other uses. These sticks were used to string tobacco and to hang the tobacco in the barn. Wood was as important then as electricity is now. (Courtesy of Velma Knight.)

Tenant farming was prevalent in the mid-1900s. This tenant house was larger than many and sat across the road from Henry and Bettie Knight's house. Farm owners furnished housing, crop supplies, and living expenses and divided the profits with the tenant according to a prearranged percentage, usually fifty-fifty. The tenant often did not have enough to carry the family over until the next year. (Courtesy of Velma Knight.)

Broadwell's Store was a place for socializing and buying goods. After a long day's work or possibly during the winter, farmers went in to have something to drink and to talk about farming, fishing, and anything else that came to mind. The store carried a variety of merchandise, from snacks to hardware. Owned originally by John Griffin, then by James Broadwell, it operated from 1903 until Broadwell's death in 2005. (Courtesy of Dick Holmes.)

Whether for jelly, grape juice, wine, or to be eaten right off the vine, grapes were a staple of most farms in the area as well as for some houses in town. Many hot afternoons have been spent preserving that fresh taste for the winter ahead. (Courtesy of Gary McConkey.)

Henry Rufus Knight, youngest son of
Henry Haywood Knight, and his bride,
Alwayne Anderson of Hayesville, pose
for their wedding picture. Anderson was a
teacher at Knightdale High School, and she
continued in that role after the wedding.
Education was her passion. At the time
of his father's death, Henry Rufus was a
small baby. (Courtesy of Velma Knight.)

Alwayne Knight
is at home with
her granddaughter
Deborah. The
Knights built a log
house across the
road from the elder
Knight's home. The
men cut pine logs,
peeled them, and
fit them together
to create a rustic
but well-built
home. Alwayne
enjoyed the rustic
look, in keeping
with her partial
Native American
ancestry. (Courtesy
of Velma Knight.)

Henry Knight loved farming and did so until he was too old to work the fields. He took great pride in growing large cantaloupes, watermelons, and pumpkins. In this photograph, Henry and his grandson Woody sit with some of his prize pumpkins. Henry took great care, even placing foil under each pumpkin to prevent damage to the underside. (Courtesy of Velma Knight.)

Henry Haywood Knight, grandson of Henry Haywood Knight, is ready to go with his parents to see his uncle Winton Anderson, who was stationed at Seymour Johnson Air Force Base in Goldsboro, in February 1944. His favorite stuffed animal, Teddy, is going on the trip as well. Some childhood habits are timeless. (Courtesy of Velma Knight.)

Besides timber and cotton, farmers produced other crops. Some grew tobacco and corn. The Knightdale area included large forests with farms in open areas. Since they were larger than those west of this area, farms farther east could have larger fields. Producing the highest yield within the confines of any farm was and still is the goal. (Authors' collections.)

The earliest tobacco barns were built of logs with mud chinking. Chinking was used to fill in the gaps between logs, making the building sturdier and better able to retain heat. The rounded structures attached to the building were where wood was burned for curing the tobacco. Fires had to be carefully tended to prevent burning the barn and the crop inside. (Courtesy of Peggy Andrews.)

Barning tobacco was gummy, hot work. Farmworkers handed bundles of three or four sticky leaves to the stringer, who tied them to the stick. After enough sticks to fill a barn were tied, they were hung in the barns for curing using a controlled wood fire. When the tobacco was cured, it was removed from the barn and sold at the local market. (Courtesy of Peggy Andrews.)

86

An employee of Pair Lumber Company works his snaking horse through the log woods. Often, the trees were too close together for a logging cart to pass through. Horses were used to pull trees out of the woods, to areas that carts could reach. Workers then loaded the carts, which took the trees to the waiting trucks. (Courtesy of Percy Pair Jr.)

James Smith (center) and his coworkers enjoy several trophies of the log woods. These raccoons will be fattened, cleaned, cooked, and served for dinner. The trick was to avoid being bitten between finding the raccoon and going home. The raccoons were often placed in barrels and grain-fed for fattening and better taste. (Courtesy of Percy Pair Jr.)

This oil-fired tobacco barn was an improvement over wood-fired barns. These structures had four heaters that had to be adjusted for successful curing. Each barn had a thermometer hanging inside, allowing the farmer to keep the temperature constant. The use of oil allowed the farmer to check the barn before going to sleep and eliminated the need to go out to stoke the fire before morning. (Courtesy of Velma Knight.)

Though Knightdale now has shops, restaurants, and secure medical services, farms exist just outside the town limit. They are an important aspect of the economy. The area is a blend of established and new lifestyles. This photograph shows a soybean field with a barn and farm equipment in the background. (Courtesy of Gary McConkey.)

Cecil Pair (left) served as a sawyer at Pair Lumber Company for many years. This 1948 photograph shows Pair and other employees at work. The sawdust cloud in the center partially obscures one man. Today's Occupational Safety and Health Administration would shudder at the lack of safety precautions and the very dangerous equipment. These dangers, and the minimal protection from the weather, make the job seem nearly unbearable to those reading this book. (Courtesy of Percy Pair Jr.)

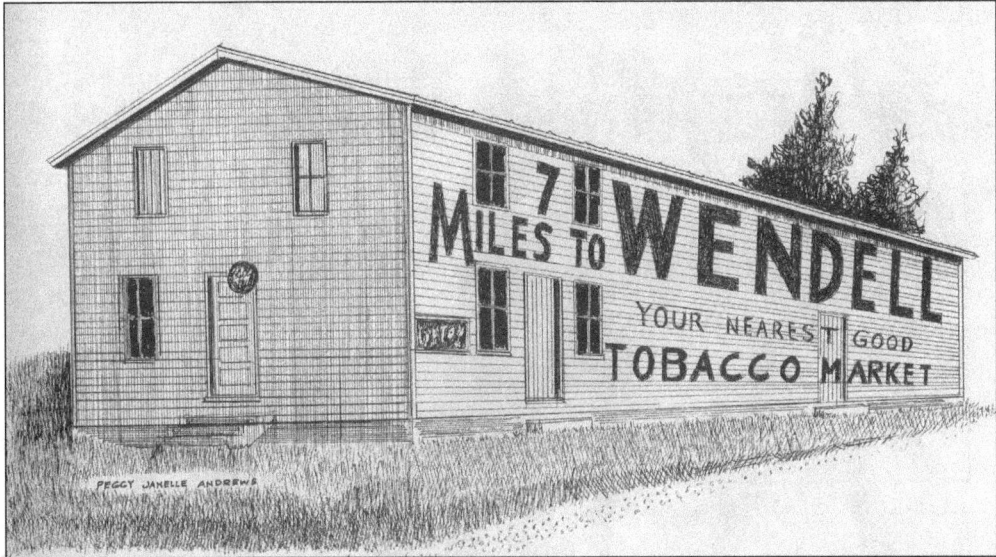

Samuel Dolphin Griffin ran a store at the corner of First Avenue and US Route 64, where the Shell Oil station stands today. Griffin sold farm supplies and other goods. He apparently also did not mind advertising for the Wendell Tobacco Market. Griffin's home was across a field to the east, so he did not have far to go to work. (Courtesy of Peggy Andrews.)

Acral M. Smith, brother of Bettie Knight, and Alma Griffin Smith, daughter of Samuel Dolphin Griffin, farmed across Tarborough Road from the sawmill. Their granddaughter Mary Ann Smith is seen here with them. They stand at a small chicken house provided for hatching chicks. The farm included tobacco and many chickens, which were raised for egg production and poultry sales, mostly to Watson Poultry on Poole Road. (Authors' collections.)

This photograph is of the James Rufus House family. Shown here are, from left to right, (seated) Dick Saintsing (father of Bettie), Bettie Saintsing House, and her husband, James Rufus House; (standing) Eddie House (son) and Ethel House (daughter). Their farm was located on the current Old Ferrell Road. (Courtesy of Christine House.)

This photograph features a snaking mule, used in logging, and a white horse, sometimes used as well. They could fit through areas that logging equipment could not, pulling trees out of the woods. The trees were cut and the limbs stripped. Loggers then loaded the carts to make the rest of the journey out of the woods. (Courtesy of Henry Poole.)

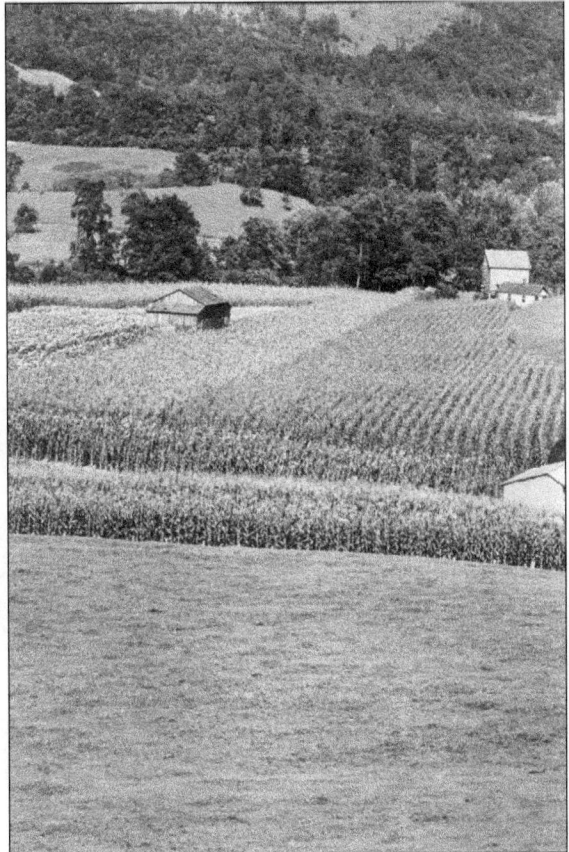

This photograph shows the rolling hills that combine with the increasing flatness of the coastal plain. In the early 20th century, this ground would have been broken up through hard work. Walking behind a mule or horse was quite different from sitting in today's air-conditioned tractors. After they lay fallow for winter, cultivating the fields was a welcome sign of spring. (Courtesy of Gary McConkey.)

Local breeder Haywood Poole owned a mammoth jackass, which he crossed with horses to produce bigger, stronger mules for logging, a popular local enterprise. In the late 1940s, when Wake County named all of its roads, Jackass Road was selected because of the local history of the animal. In the late 1980s, due to public sentiment, the county changed the name to Old Knight Road. (Courtesy of Henry Poole.)

Logging was more hazardous in the 1930s than it is today. This 1932 photograph shows Percy Pair Sr. on his Fordson steel-wheeled tractor, hauling a logging cart to even thicker woods. Horses and mules pulled log carts out of the woods. The huge logs were a product of the local soil, which promoted pine tree growth. (Courtesy of Percy Pair Jr.)

Sometimes, drivers had to be innovative. Such is the case here. In order to unload lumber, Tobe Tyler situates the truck so that it will tilt, causing the load to shift and slide off the truck. Lacking dump trucks, this method saved time and labor. This truck is from Pair Lumber Company. (Courtesy of Percy Pair Jr.)

Surely, this lumber truck has all it can carry. After lumber was processed at the sawmill, useable boards were ready to be carried to the depot for shipment, or perhaps to stores that sold lumber. Another possibility is that the sawmill sold the lumber to customers, and the driver was preparing to deliver it. (Courtesy of Knightdale Historical Society.)

Now aging, this Railroad Street building was one of the busiest places in town in the 1920s and 1930s, when it was James Shouthall's livery stable. The business sold and traded horses and mules for work or pleasure. According to Alene Wilder, who lived across the street, the youngest son, John, sat on the fence and never missed anything that happened at the livery. (Authors' collections.)

Williams Dairy was the first Grade A dairy in the area. Charles Williams and his son Sidney sold milk and cream from the establishment. For many years, Sidney delivered to private homes throughout the rural area and to neighboring towns and Raleigh. The farm is still in the Williams family. (Authors' collections.)

Eight

DO WHAT?

With the end of World War II, a new era dawned. Jobs and the transportation to reach them were available. Good pay for that work was available as well. Education levels rose, and technology improved in all fields. Better jobs and better pay allowed more free time—a new luxury. In Knightdale, much of this time was spent improving the lives of the citizens.

As people saw the town as a good place to live, Knightdale responded by adding services. The town provided some amenities and volunteers established many others. These residents' time, talents, and, often, money made life better—whether through emergency services, parks, schools, or other areas of life.

Dr. Rupert Ryan Weathers, the second town doctor, practiced in the area for 32 years. According to the Knightdale Historical Society, he was born near Wendell in 1897. A graduate of the Medical College of Virginia, Weathers served as mayor from 1942 to 1948. He was known for his calm demeanor. (Courtesy of Town of Knightdale.)

Wiley Robertson Jr. and his sister Doris, approximately seven and five years old respectively, enjoy a summer day, complete with a tasty apple. What could be better than no school, someone to play with, and a treat for munching? They seem to be viewing the town from a somewhat high vantage point. (Courtesy of Doris Robertson Anthony.)

John Carlisle Stalvey came to town in August 1939 to replace an ailing John Davis as pharmacist. He was mayor from 1948 to 1949. Stalvey had to resign the $5-per-month mayor's job in 1949 when he bought his home at 801 North First Avenue, because it was just outside the town limit. Many of the photographs in this publication are products of his efforts. (Courtesy of Town of Knightdale.)

Lewis Parrish (fourth from left) built a radio station in his parents' home when he was in high school. After graduation, he worked with Wynne Radio in Raleigh, was station engineer for WPTF in Raleigh, and built WETC in Wendell. In addition, Parrish built several Voice of America stations in other parts of the world. (Courtesy of John Bruce Parrish.)

Early-1950s fashion is on display in this photograph of the class of 1952. The bobby socks are pushed down the same amount, and saddle oxfords seem to be a prerequisite for going to school. Among the students are twins Jerry Allen (second row, second from right) and Jack Allen (third row, third from left), who seem to be dressed alike. Note how the boys' hairstyles foreshadow those to come in the early 2000s. Variations of these girls' hairstyles are still seen today, as is the desire to have the latest look. Photographs of senior classes today usually involve hundreds of students. (Authors' collections.)

Knightdale Medical Center was financed by the brainstorm of Ashley Wilder and other investors who bought stock in it. It opened in January 1960, with Dr. Norman Hornstein as the first occupant. He was the town's third doctor and the first to have only one office with plenty of patients. Currently, Dr. Rajendra Nigalye occupies the office. The building also hosts a food distribution and community care program. (Courtesy of Knightdale Historical Society.)

The first brick Knightdale School on Ridge Street is gone, and the new Knightdale Elementary stands in its place. Population growth and an aging building brought about the change. The school has a bus driveway on one side and a carpool driveway on the other. Street parking is available on Ridge Street. This school is one of four elementary schools serving Knightdale today. (Authors' collections.)

Eugene Field Harper was born in Laurel (now Louisburg), North Carolina, and came to Knightdale as an adult, working at Robertson & Keith General Merchandise Store. In 1935, he married Lillian Robertson. Having graduated from Campbell College in 1930, he sought a tool machinist degree from North Carolina State College, receiving it in 1942. His degree served him well, as he became a test machinist for American Machinery Foundry. He served as mayor from 1949 to 1962 and from 1964 to 1976. His terms were interrupted when his job required that he work temporarily out of state. Lillian died in 1979, and Eugene married Lois Faison Hollifield in 1982. As evidenced by his long tenure as mayor, he was considered an excellent leader. Harper's legacy is the completed water and sewer systems. Harper Park was named in his memory. (Courtesy of Town of Knightdale.)

A truckload of lumber is leaving the log woods. The model year of the truck is not known, but the license plate displays the year 1950. The lumber will go to the planer mill for planing, a process that smoothes the boards for use in building. The next stop will be someone's new home, as the area continues to grow. (Courtesy of Percy Pair Jr.)

The Wiley Robertson family is pictured in a reenactment of a photograph taken years earlier. The family spirit carries on, no matter the year. Shown here are, from left to right, (first row) Cassie, Wiley Jr., and Rachel; (second row) Gladys, Wiley Sr., Rosa, Blanche, Doris, and George. (Courtesy of Doris Robertson Anthony.)

The Ford Model T seen at the right in this image was one of the newer ways to go into town to conduct necessary business. People could park and go to the pharmacy, with its post office inside, and easily visit the bank next door. Multiple-use establishments seem to have been popular much longer than might be imagined. (Courtesy of John Bruce Parrish.)

The third freestanding post office was at 207 First Avenue. As the town grew, more capacity was needed for mail services and for parking. Another route had been added by that time, so mail carriers and customers were competing for street parking. This location included a parking lot and easier access for customers. (Courtesy of Knightdale Historical Society.)

In the 1960s, fire departments were mostly composed of volunteers. The men in this photograph answered fire calls day and night. Firefighters who worked in Raleigh could respond to calls when they were off work. The loud siren mounted on the fire station called everyone within hearing range to help. The large structure at left is the water tower. (Courtesy of Knightdale Historical Society.)

The business district and homes that were destroyed in the 1940 fire were rebuilt. This photograph gives a view down First Avenue, with its cement sidewalks. The hope was that rebuilding with brick would help prevent another destructive event. The Bank of Wendell was flanked by the barbershop and, farther down, Robertson's Store, with the other side next to Knightdale Pharmacy (pictured). (Courtesy of John Stalvey.)

This 1955 Knightdale Pharmacy Christmas card is a reminder of days gone by. Pharmacist John Stalvey (left) holds a bottle of medicine, grill operator Robert Clark (center) holds a hot dog, and Fred Mangum holds a drink. Fresh slices of pie on the counter and sundries in the cabinets on the wall are for sale. Interestingly, the hood over the grill looks very much like today's models. (Courtesy of Knightdale Historical Society.)

Percy Pair Jr. (left), David Pope (center), and John Bruce Parrish stand beside Knightdale Fire Department Rural Truck No. 1. The department served both the town proper and the surrounding area for many years. The fire department had made much progress by the time this 1970s photograph was taken. Going from no equipment to multiple trucks in a little over 20 years was quite an accomplishment. In addition, when the siren sounded, many more people were available to answer the call, no matter the hour. The department has continued to grow and has divided into the Eastern Wake Fire Department, serving the area outside of town, and Knightdale Fire Department, serving the area within the ever-growing town limit and its citizenry, numbering in the thousands. (Courtesy of John Bruce Parrish.)

Shown here is Wendell-Knightdale Airport, previously Wake County Airport and now Raleigh East Airport. It was begun by Joe Thomas Knott in 1965. He tells of laying out the runway with a friend who wanted to move his airplane to eastern Wake County. The friend had several children in diapers, so he and Knott used tobacco sticks and diapers to mark the runway. (Courtesy of Knightdale Historical Society.)

The Knightdale Heritage Council was formed in October 1984. Mayor Billy Wilder appointed John Stalvey, William Wilder Sr., Peggy Andrews, Edna Kropp, and Anne Hildebrand, and they began the work of collecting the town's history. They were the foundation for the Knightdale Historical Society. As many citizens have died, so would have the history without the efforts of these individuals. The work they produced will continue to benefit the town in a museum to be developed at a later date. (Courtesy of Peggy Andrews.)

Knightdale N.C.
1927
62 YEARS
1989
Incorporated
March 9, 1927

Ashley Wilder lived most of his childhood on Oaks Plantation on Clifton Road. As an adult, he was a farmer, grocery clerk, merchant, salvage company operator, and wood-stove salesman. He helped to organize the fire department and to develop the first medical center. A visionary, Wilder constantly looked for ways to help the town prosper. He served as mayor from 1962 to 1964. (Courtesy of Town of Knightdale.)

This photograph shows the Knightdale Volunteer Fire Department in 1978. Small towns did not have paid firefighters; consequently, residents rushed from homes or work to the fire station to man trucks that carried everything they needed, including water. Annual barbecue dinners raised funds for new equipment. As larger businesses, such as Wake Stone, moved into town, they helped furnish equipment. (Courtesy of John Bruce Parrish.)

Luther Faison was one of the earliest developers in the area. The Sidney Faison ancestral home stands on Smithfield Road in front of the first group of new homes in town. In the 1960s, Faison developed the Weathers Dairy pasture into Faison Drive, Park Avenue, and Smithfield Road, the first sizeable area of new brick homes in Knightdale. (Authors' collections.)

Phyllis and Larry Addelton bought Knightdale Seafood and Bar-B-Q in 1988. The building had been Cooper's Service Station. It was the only full-service restaurant in town. A line stretching across the restaurant yard was quite common on Friday evenings, and the takeout section was crowded as well. In 2001, the restaurant moved one mile east, to a location with greater capacity both indoors and out. (Courtesy of Knightdale Historical Society.)

Zebbie Robison began his career with Knightdale Seafood & Bar-B-Q as a student assistant. Since 1994, he has continued cooking and chopping barbecue for the restaurant and will soon celebrate his 20th work anniversary. Robison, regarded as one of the best barbecue chefs in eastern North Carolina, is a fixture in the restaurant. His student assistant certificate hangs with this picture on the restaurant wall. His advice is to use green hickory wood for cooking and not to experiment with the sauce in an established restaurant. Regular customers will definitely know the difference. Over the years, he has chopped thousands of pounds of meat. Thank goodness, technology has made the work easier. Chopping is now mechanized, and hickory smoke flavors the meat while gas cooks it. Robison says that he stays in the job because he enjoys it and because the people are nice. (Courtesy of Phyllis Addelton.)

Knightdale Heritage Council members Maggie Eddins (third from left), Anne Hildebrand (second from right), and Lewis Parrish (far right), who appears ready to capture the moment with his camera, are accompanied by three unidentified people as they explore a cave just east of town. It has served as a point of interest for exploration for over 100 years. Knightdale and much of eastern Wake County are home to rock formations and underground granite, known to some as the Rolesville Shelf. The council members were known for providing little-known facts from the past. Many people did and still do ride by this area daily without knowing that this formation exists. The council gathered information and pictures in the late 1980s through the mid-1990s. Its work provided the foundation for this book. (Courtesy of Knightdale Historical Society.)

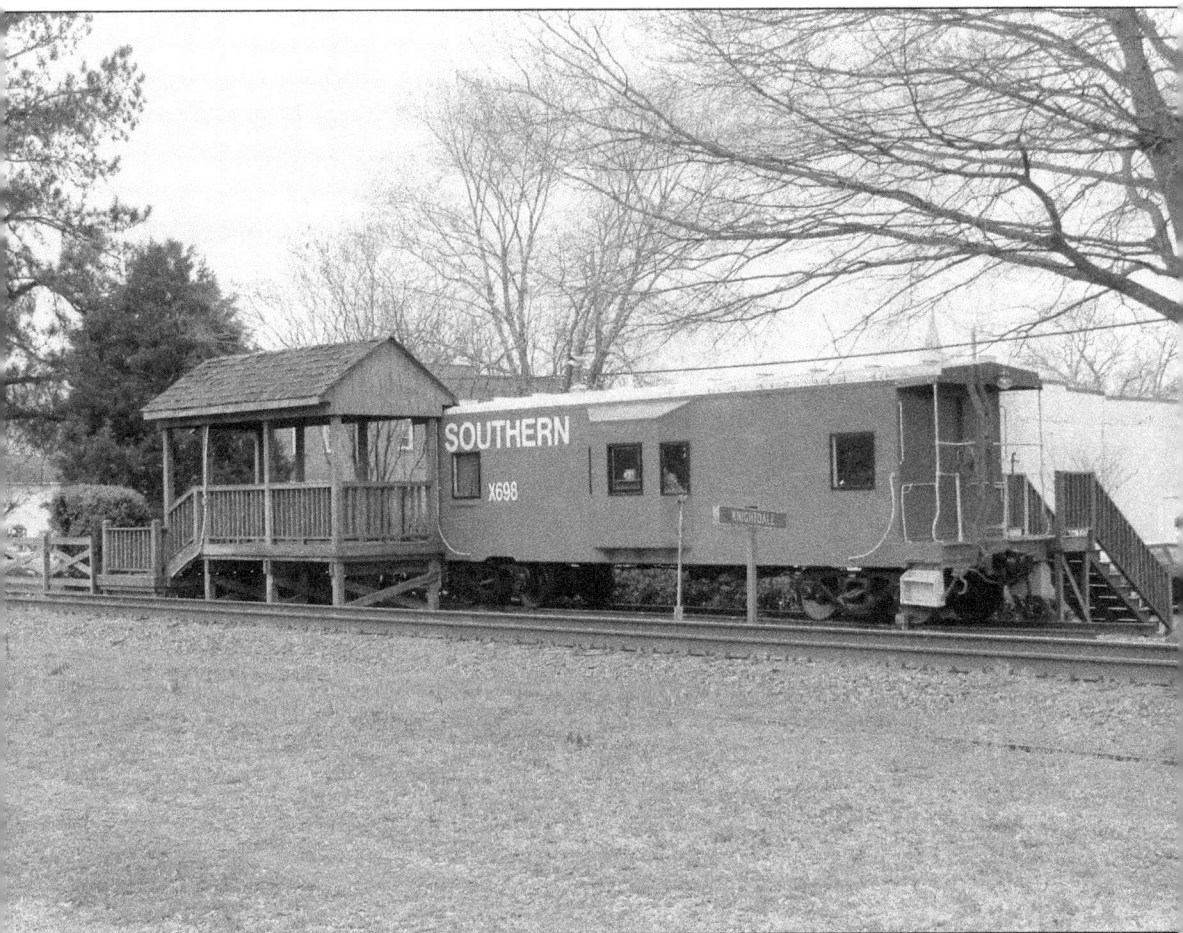

A repainted caboose sits where the depot stood shortly after Knightdale began. The railroad sign indicating the town name reminds visitors of that beginning. First Avenue is a tribute to the town's heritage. Many of the original homes remain occupied as well. The makeover of First Avenue helps immerse newcomers in town history. Residents whose heritage is represented in the town are amazed at how the spirit of the people aided in the town's development. Entrepreneurs, farmers, determined women, and countless volunteers are responsible for the sights that greet new residents and visitors. The makeover of First Avenue, a huge undertaking, is moving the town into the next phase of its life. People can stop and sit near the bakery or stake out a place for the Christmas parade. At a time when many worried that First Avenue would be forgotten, it continues to offer its unique personality. (Authors' collections.)

Built by Billy Wilder, Wilder's Nursery was on First Avenue, where it served the community with plants and trees for many years. The open land in the lower left of the photograph is now Knightdale Station Town Park. The upper part of the photograph shows how the railroad makes an S curve through the town. (Authors' collections.)

Built in the early 1970s, Green Pines Baptist Church has been an integral part of the Knightdale community, especially the Barclay Downs and Green Pines areas. It was one of the earlier new churches after the building of the present Knightdale Baptist Church. While hard to imagine now, when it was built, the church was considered to be remote in relation to the town. (Authors' collections.)

In 1977, with town funds and a grant, Knightdale's first town hall became a reality. Years of planning and saving paid off with the construction of this building and its parking lot. It housed the police department and the library. One room was designated for council meetings and other necessary gatherings as well as serving as the polling place for elections. (Authors' collections.)

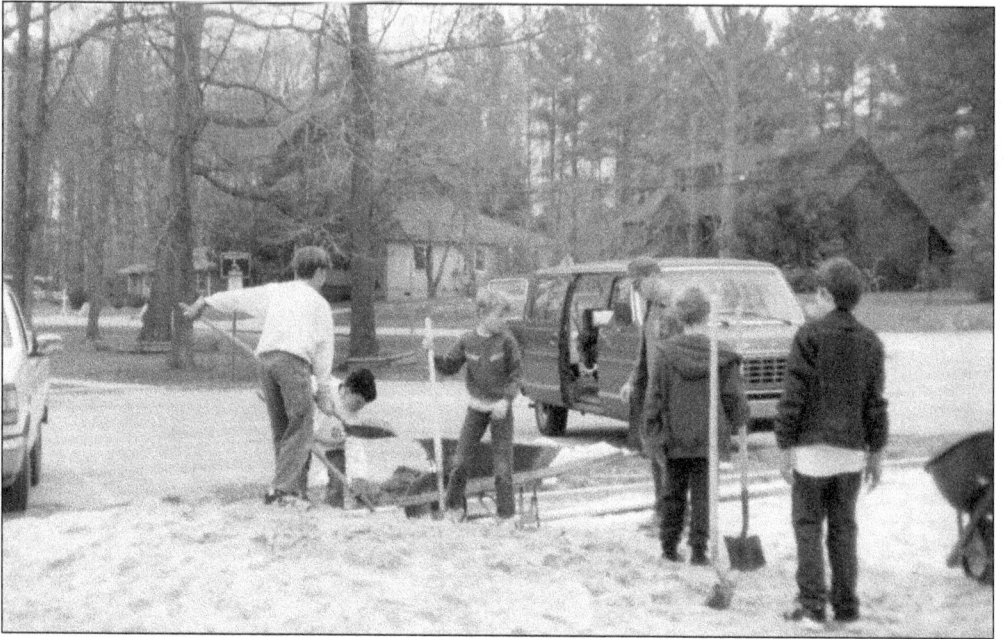

A local Boy Scout troop helps to spread sand in the sandbox at Harper Park, which opened in the 1980s on the grounds of the first town hall. While the park was built with grant money, much of the labor was volunteer. These boys and their leader are an example of that giving spirit. (Courtesy of Knightdale Historical Society.)

Hodge Road Elementary School was the second elementary school among the four that are now in Knightdale. Due to the rapid influx of new residents, it follows the year-round calendar, as do many elementary and middle schools in Wake County. It features a parent academy, which helps parents become partners in the education of their children. (Authors' collections.)

Nine

INDEPENDENCE DAY

Knightdale finally became independent. With local jobs and exciting places to eat and shop, the slow little town was given fabulous new opportunities. Farsighted leaders realized that people wanted a small-town atmosphere and safety with city comforts. Churches expanded to meet the spiritual needs of the people, and major shopping and recreational opportunities became available.

True to the heritage of Knightdale's educational focus, a strong emphasis on facilities is evident in the construction of new schools. Each day, residents have the chance to enjoy new vocational, educational, recreational, shopping, and religious experiences. Public safety officials, both paid and volunteer, assure that citizens reside in a safe environment.

The earliest franchise restaurant was Hardee's, a well-established fast-food chain from Rocky Mount. The Knightdale location, built in 1986, was located at the corner of Smithfield Road and Knightdale Boulevard. It was the first business to select an out parcel of the town's first shopping center, Knightdale Crossing, as its location. It has become a morning meeting place for senior citizens and retirees. (Authors' collections.)

Knightdale's first large shopping area was Knightdale Crossing, at the corner of Knightdale Boulevard and Smithfield Road. Built in 1986, it featured Winn-Dixie, Davy's, Revco, and Hardee's. For the first time, residents could buy a full line of groceries in their own town. The gin and sawmill had given way to tobacco that, in turn, gave way to commercial space, which continues to evolve and grow. (Authors' collections.)

William A. Wilder Jr., a lifelong resident of Knightdale, served as mayor from 1976 to 1992 and helped usher in commercial growth. Development often brought disagreement, so the mayor faced the challenge of keeping the meetings peaceful—no small job. As with other mayors in small towns, the pay was little, usually under $30 a month. Public service was done out of duty and love of place. (Courtesy of Town of Knightdale.)

Maplewood, built in the early 1980s, was one of the earlier subdivisions in town. It, and others like it, challenged the town government to learn how to grow well and carefully. It continues to thrive, providing beautiful, convenient housing for long-term and new residents. One unique feature is the seamless joining of Maplewood and Pebblebrook Subdivision streets. (Authors' collections.)

Schneider Electric, a green-energy company, occupies East Point on East Knightdale Boulevard. It has proven to be a boost to the economy, offering jobs and supporting the community. According to its website, Schneider works to "support local, national and international nonprofit agencies that focus on education, health and human services, the arts and culture, and social and civic programs." (Authors' collections.)

Another religious denomination is represented on Old Faison Road. The Knightdale Church of God has been a part of the community since the 1960s, and it continues to serve a thriving congregation. One of the church's more recent technological additions are vimeos (blogged videos), which welcome visitors to the church through its website. (Authors' collections.)

In addition to the 1940 fire, Knightdale has seen other calamities. This photograph shows the aftermath of Hurricane Fran, which struck on the night of September 5, 1996. The entire town looked like a logging camp, as residents began cutting away trees from homes and cars. Under this pile of trees is a Plymouth Reliant K-car, which, like the town's spirit, suffered only a small dent. (Authors' collections.)

A partnership among Wake County Schools, Wake County Parks and Recreation, and the Town of Knightdale enabled the Forestville Road Elementary School to be built on this campus. Students share space, allowing more versatility in physical education and the arts. Growth necessitates creativity in providing for a community's needs. (Authors' collections.)

Again, the town grew and needed a bigger post office. The fourth location was on Smithfield Road at Railroad Street, where residents often stopped to chat with friends. Since the building was across from the train track, people hurried across the tracks either going to or returning from the post office. Why? Most trains had at least 200 cars and moved very slowly because of three in-town crossings. (Courtesy of John Stalvey.)

The town's new recreational center is attached to Forestville Road Elementary School, one of three elementary schools that serve Knightdale. The center includes programs for youth, along with craft programs, such as pottery classes. The building also serves as a polling place and hosts bridge clubs and arts programs. (Authors' collections.)

120

The more recent town sign is brightened by the landscaping formerly provided by John Bruce Parrish and now performed by Two Thumbs Up Garden Club. Parrish helped create the fire department and served on the town board for many years. He can be seen in the 1980s fire department photograph (see page 105). (Courtesy of Knightdale Historical Society.)

The Knightdale Chamber of Commerce occupies the original town hall. The chamber has gone from merely being a body that met wherever it could in 1973, to having a phone in the business of the executive director in 1981, to now having a home, three full-time employees, and over 400 members. It promotes Knightdale as a good place to live, work, and raise a family. (Authors' collections.)

Knightdale United Methodist Church has outgrown its First Avenue location. From bringing Oaky Grove into its congregation in 1917, to relocating to Forestville Road (pictured), Knightdale United Methodist has continued to help the town grow. The First Avenue site now houses Northside Community Church. (Authors' collections.)

As the population grows, so does the number of religious denominations. The most recent is the Church of Jesus Christ of Latter-day Saints, which has a church on Forestville Road. Some denominations begin by using the high school facilities, some by using storefronts, and some by using the Lions Club. All add to the texture of Knightdale. (Authors' collections.)

Much of Wake County has become urban, so Knightdale has worked hard to preserve its natural and environmentally sensitive spaces. Pictured here is the Knightdale Environmental Park, located on the former Knight property and donated to the town by Wake Stone. The peace and serenity encourage visitors to pause, reflect, and renew. (Authors' collections.)

A slightly elevated walkway allows people to enjoy the environmental park without harming its sensitive elements. Hikers can take photographs of the beautiful surroundings and even get a shot of unusual wildlife if they're quiet enough and still enough to blend into the area. Birds, foxes, rabbits, wild turkeys, and many other animals inhabit the area. (Authors' collections.)

The present Knightdale Town Hall was opened on October 6, 1996, on Steeple Square Court, on a tract owned by Acral Smith in 1900. Since that time, three more buildings have been added to the campus: East Regional Library; Knightdale Public Safety, which includes fire, rescue, and police; and East Wake television studio. (Authors' collections.)

From one officer working out of his home to a 26-officer department, the town has maintained the goal of providing the best police and fire protection. The number of officers included here reflects just the police department. In addition, paid firefighters and paramedics are available to care for those in need. (Authors' collections.)

124

East Regional Library occupies the same campus as the current town hall and public safety center. Having begun as a library to service the small community, it now serves much of eastern Wake County. It is one of the large library centers providing a substantial circulation and access to technology. (Authors' collections.)

The current Knightdale Post Office (shown here) is a leap in modernity from the method of receiving mail by rail. Located on McKnight Drive, it provides full service to the town's residents. Before the 1990s, citizens would have had difficulty imagining such a service, complete with ample parking. Once having only one rural route, the local postal service now has about eight daily routes. (Courtesy of Knightdale Historical Society.)

Knightdale has a high school again. The first high school operated from 1926 through 1965. From the fall of 1965 until the fall of 2004, students went to Vaiden Whitley and, later, East Wake. The new Knightdale High School opened in the fall of 2004 and features a three-story design. With their armored Knight mascot, the Knights are proud to have their own identity and home. (Authors' collections.)

Knightdale High has had its own baseball fields since the school opened in August 2004. Knightdale High and Forestville Road Elementary are on the same campus. According to Wake County Public Schools, funds for the schools came from the school system, the Town of Knightdale, and Wake County Parks and Recreation, which enabled the installation of athletic fields when the school was built. (Authors' collections.)

126

The latest town park already has a children's playground in place. Appropriately, the children can play on a train engine designed just for them. Knightdale's agricultural heritage is reflected in the barn and silo, complete with a cow resting in the field. The construction materials present in both photographs indicate that work continues at this site. In the past, Knightdale has had two ball fields, and more teams than existing facilities. When the park opened in late September 2013, more fields were available, along with adequate parking. In addition, the park is adjacent to the Knightdale location of the YMCA planned for 2015. (Both, authors' collections.)

Visit us at
arcadiapublishing.com

www.ingramcontent.com/pod-product-compliance
Lightning Source LLC
Chambersburg PA
CBHW050643110426
42813CB00007B/1898